My ANOVA
Sous Vide
Home Kitchen
Cookbook

100 SIMPLE AND DELICIOUS GOURMET RECIPES AND PRO TIPS FOR BEGINNERS AND EXPERTS

BY

JESSICA MICHAEL

Bay City Press

BAY CITY PRESS
SANTA MONICA, CA.

Customer Reviews

"My first experience with sous vide was a huge success, I made the steak recipe from this book for some friends and not only were they surprised that I'd made it myself, but they didn't believe how until I showed them the book. Total game changer for people how love gourmet food." – Julie M.

"Nutrition is very important to me and it's one of the reasons I decided to try sous vide cooking in the first place. I had read this cooking method retained a lot of nutrients so having the nutritional information included for each recipe was an added bonus. I'm just getting started and the book got me up and running immediately." – Anne B.

"This book was very illuminating to me. I'll never go back to cooking the same way again. Meals are simply so much more flavorful than I was accustomed, and it makes perfect sense why cooking sous vide would retain otherwise lost nutrients." – David B.

"This 'gourmet' product intimidated me until I got this book. It quickly helped me understand the simplicity behind the process. Every recipe is a winner and the book offers a huge variety of meals. It's been a very tasty adventure... I sound like 'Bill & Ted's Excellent Adventure' Thanks dudes!" – Amanda C.

"I didn't know what to do with the anova so it sat in my cupboard for months until a friend gave me this book. The recipes are delicious, but more importantly, very easy to follow! I've already made steaks, salmon, pudding, and some very tasty egg dishes that impressed my friends and myself." – Jamie O.

Legal Notice

All content herein represents the author's own experiences and opinions. The information written, illustrated and presented in this book is for the purpose of entertainment only.

Although we are big fans, neither the author, nor Bay City Press, are associated with the manufacturer of the Anova Sous Vide Circulator.

The author does not assume any liability for the use of or inability to use any or all of the information contained in this book and does not accept responsibility for any type of loss or damage that may be experienced by the user as the result of activities occurring from the use of any information in this book. Use the information at your own risk. The author reserves the right to make changes he or she deems required to future versions of the publication to maintain accuracy.

Table Of Contents

1

Why You Need This Book!

Save Time with Our Illustrated Quick-Start Guide

Our illustrated quick-start guide gets you cooking in no time. Not only does this book offer a huge variety of delicious recipes but also reveals the secret methods of proper sous vide cooking. It gives you everything you need, from proper preparation to cooking those five-star restaurant quality meals that also save time, money and energy. Best of all, your dishes will come out perfect every time. This is why top chefs from all over the world have been using the sous vide cooking method for decades.

Unbiased Real-World Instructions NOT in the Manual

This comprehensive guide to sous vide cooking with your Anova sous vide goes beyond the manual to provide you with everything you need to know to get the most out of your Anova. We will go into depth about the science of sous vide cooking and show you the ideal methods to prepare anything you can think of. We also offer creative tips for preparing and seasoning foods before you cook, and practical methods for serving and storing your foods after you finish cooking. This valuable book really does teach you everything you need to know to help you use your Anova sous vide like a pro.

Pro Tips to Get More Out of Your Anova

We've got tips to take your sous vide skills to the next level, and you won't find these pro tips in the Anova manual. Our tips will ensure you get the best results from your sous vide, so you can get started making impressive restaurant quality dishes from day one. These tips will also help you avoid common mistakes people make when using sous vide that can kill your meal. You'll be using your sous vide like a professional chef after learning these tips.

100 Amazing Recipes You Won't Find in The Manual or Other Cookbooks

We want to save you time, so we put together 100 amazing recipes. Our recipes allow you to prepare food with your sous vide for every meal and occasion. You won't have to go to the bookstore, nor search high & low to find great tasting recipes. You won't find these unique and tasty recipes anywhere else. You'll have it all quickly accessible in this simple, illustrated book.

Learn Sous Vide Like A Pro by Avoiding Common Mistakes

This book will cover everything you need to know to use your Anova. You'll learn everything—including what tools to use, water levels, and all the functions of your sous vide. This device, once only used in restaurants, will make healthy, delicious and nutrient-retaining food, right in your home kitchen, turning you into a gourmet chef. Your friends and family will be surprised, impressed and feel very welcome to dinner.

2

All About Sous Vide

What is Sous Vide?

You're probably wondering what sous vide (pronounced sue veed) cooking actually is. Its technique cooks food at incredibly precise temperatures in a water bath. Food is placed in sealed bags to ensure it doesn't get wet. The device is attached to the side of the cooking container where it heats up and circulates water, which remains at a consistent temperature throughout the entire cooking process. Sous vide allows you to cook your dishes evenly and at the exact temperature you want. This allows you to get consistent results.

The precise temperatures allow moisture and nutrients to stay in your food. Steak cooked with other methods can lose as much as 40% of its volume as it dries out.

Sous vide cooks food at its ideal core temperature. It's the point where food is warm enough to kill harmful pathogens. Cooking at core temperature means that your food won't be overdone if you don't take it out at the right moment or underdone either. When you cook using conventional methods like in an oven the food cooks at much higher temperatures than the food's core. You risk overcooking the food even if you take it out a couple minutes late.

Cooking sous vide also means you don't have to stand over the food and keep checking it. You can simply place the food in the water bath, set a timer, and do whatever you'd like while you wait. It simplifies the entire cooking process for you.

Who Uses Sous Vide

All different types of people use sous vide. It's been popular in restaurants across the world for decades. Many of the best restaurants in the world use sous vide to create delicious food. Sous vide was the restaurant industry's best-kept secret for a long time.

Now, thanks to advances in technology, more affordable pricing and smaller units, sous vide machines are available for home use. Business professionals, busy mothers, millennials, baby boomers, and everyone in between are using sous vide. It's perfect for anyone looking to make an incredible meal and save time.

Brief History

The origins of sous vide can be traced all the way back to Benjamin Thompson in 1799. He made a machine that used heated air to drive potatoes. He placed a piece of Martin in the machine for a few hours to see if he could roast the meat but failed. His maids, however, decided to leave the meat in the machine overnight and to their amazement, the meat was perfectly cooked. Although the machine used heat instead of water, the process was quite similar.

The first big innovations for modern sous vide cooking came about in the mid-1960s. French and American engineers developed a method for creating pressure on food through vacuum sealing. It was developed as well to industrially preserve food. The engineers found that the method concentrated the flavors of food and improved its texture. The technique has been dubbed Cryovacking. The term sous vide is actually French for under vacuum.

In 1974 French chef Georges Prallus started vacuum sealing foie gras for cooking. The chef wanted to find a way to keep the expensive food from losing so much weight during the cooking process. Traditionally, foie gras loses about 50% when cooked but the newly developed technique only lost 5%. It improves the texture and fat content as well.

Food scientist Bruno Goussalt started experimenting with the technique and over time created guidelines for the ideal temperature and cooking time for a variety of foods. He went on to serve sous vide cooked meals to first class patrons of Air France.

What Can I Cook Using Sous Vide?

You can cook many things using your sous vide, however, the most common dish people use it for are meat, fish and vegetables. Chefs from all over the world experiment with the boundaries of sous vide and make eggs, rice, and an assortment of desserts using it. The technique is incredibly versatile, allowing you to create a large variety of meals, side dishes and desserts.

What Other Tools Do I Need?

There are some simple tools you'll need to use with your sous vide. The first is sealable bags. You have a few options to go with including vacuum-sealed bags, reusable silicone bags, mason jars, and resealable (zip-lock) plastic bags. Vacuum sealed bags will offer the best results because they remove more air from the bag than any other method, and vacuum sealing is a great way to store leftovers. Reusable silicone bags are a good alternative. The bags are made from non-toxic silica and are dishwasher safe. Mason jars are a great choice for fruits and vegetables and are also non-toxic. Zip-lock bags are a fast and easy container and work best for shorter cooking times because they won't maintain their seal for as long as vacuum-sealed bags, but as long as they're BPA free, they are safe to use. You should always check a company's website to find out the exact information on the bags.

Many people worry that cooking food at such a low temperature won't be safe to eat, but sous vide cooking is designed to cook every food to its exact ideal temperature. Depending on what you want to cook, you will choose your perfect temperature and time setting, but in general, food cooked at low temperatures, like fish, should only be cooked for short periods of time to preserve flavor and texture, while foods cooked for long periods of time, like fall-off-the-bone baby back ribs, need to be cooked at high temperatures to prevent bacteria growth.

You will also need clips or weights to make sure your food bags stay submerged. You can buy food grade steel weights to place in the bag with your food. Stainless steel cutlery works as a weight as well. Use clips to attach the bag to the side of the container. You can also clip weights to the outside of the bag to keep it submerged.

What Are the Health Benefits of Sous Vide?

Sous vide cooking has many health benefits that other methods of cooking don't have. The added flavor that comes with sous vide cooking means you need to add little to no fat and/or salt in your food. Food maintains more vitamins and minerals with sous vide cooking. The high temperature involved with traditional cooking methods kills vitamins and mineral content in food. Some vitamins are water-soluble, so they leach out of food as they cook, but that doesn't happen with the sous vide. Foods maintain the majority of their juices and vitamins because they never get heated above their core temperature, and the water never goes above the boiling point. Food never directly interacts with oxygen, heat, or water as it does in the traditional cooking method. These elements can kill the nutrients in your food. When you sous vide food, it stays perfectly safe in its bag.

3

How to Use Your Anova

1. SEASON YOUR FOOD

2. PLACE FOOD IN A BAG OR MASON JAR

3. SUBMERGE FOOD INTO POT. USE TONGS IF WATER IS ALREADY HOT.

How to Get Started in 2 Minutes

Getting started with your Anova Sous vide couldn't be easier. The Anova uses simple controls that take the guesswork out of getting started in minutes. Remove the sous vide unit from the box and attach it to a cooking pot with the adjustable knob. Plug in the unit and you will see the control panel featuring two LED displays. The top display tells you the current temperature and the lower indicates the temperature setting you will choose. To the right of the temperature display is a button which allows you to set the timer, so you can easily keep track of how long you've been cooking. This is especially helpful for foods cooked for long periods of time. Below the display itself you will notice the blue temperature setting wheel. Simply roll the wheel up or down to set your desired temperature. At the bottom of the display is the start button. Press the start button and your Anova will begin heating and circulating the water.

DISPLAY SETTINGS:

DISPLAY FUNCTIONING:

1) Hold Start Button for 8 Seconds and Timer Button will Appear.

2) Press Timer Button and 'Chosen Temperature' display will Convert to a Timer.

Current Temperature

Chosen Temperature

Bluetooth Connection

Start Button

Temperature & Timer Control

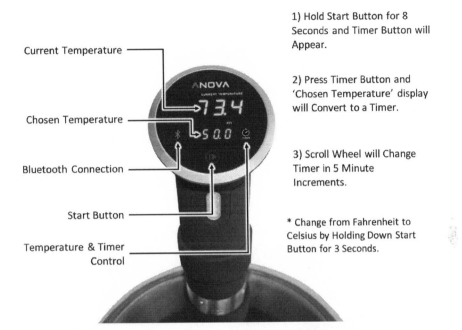

3) Scroll Wheel will Change Timer in 5 Minute Increments.

* Change from Fahrenheit to Celsius by Holding Down Start Button for 3 Seconds.

You can change the temperature display from Fahrenheit to Celsius by holding the start button for three seconds. If you want to change back simply hold the button for another three seconds.

To set the timer, hold the start button for eight seconds. The timer button will appear next to the lower display. Press the timer button, and the lower display will switch to a timer. You can then set the time by scrolling up and down on the scroll wheel which will change the timer in five-minute increments. Hit the start button to begin cooking.

Fill the container with enough water to be above the minimum fill line on the cooker, but not more than the maximum line.

Season your food however you'd like. Place the food you've chosen to cook in your bag of choice or mason jar. Submerge the bag or jar in the water once it's preheated. Feel free to use a pair of tongs to submerge the food if the water is hot.

Water Levels

It's important to keep the water in between the minimum and maximum fill line. If the water is below the minimum fill line, the water won't circulate around the food properly. The food won't cook evenly because of this, and you could end up with undercooked food. If you go above the maximum fill line, the water could overflow out of the container and damage your sous vide.

Keep Water Levels Above Minimum Fill-Line to Avoid Undercooked Food

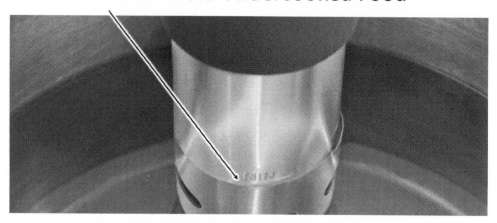

When to Use Different Temperature Settings

Using different temperature settings is great for advanced users. It's a good technique to use for meat. You can cook the meat for about eight hours at 120°F and then raise it to the normal temperature to finish it off. This makes the meat even more tender than usual.

How to Cook Vegetables

Vegetables cook at a higher temperature than meat, so it's important to use the right bag. You should avoid using re-sealable plastic bags because they tend to start melting at around 158°F. That's lower than the necessary temperature to cook vegetables. You can use reusable silicone bags, mason jars, or vacuum bags. Make sure the vacuum bags you buy are built to withstand higher temperatures.

Attach the Unit to a Cooking Pot using the Lower Adjustable Knob

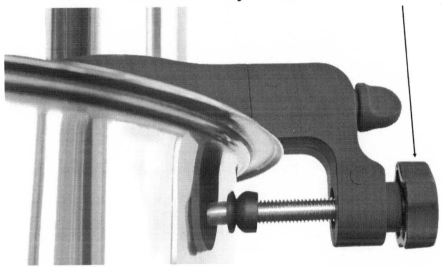

Containers

You have many options when it comes to containers to use with your ANOVA precision cooker. You can use glass, steel, plastic, ceramic, and many more. If it's a container used for cooking, it will most likely work for sous vide cooking. Some people turn coolers into containers for their sous vide. The most important thing is to find a container that is just big enough to fit whatever you're cooking. You don't want a container that's too big because you'll need to heat a lot of excess water. This forces the precision cooker to work harder than it needs to, which raises your electric bill. The container also needs to allow for enough water flow around the food, so the sous vide can work properly. Always use a container that can withstand the heat of at least 212°F, which is the boiling point of water.

Adjust the Position of the Cooker Higher or Lower Using this Adjustable Knob.

Bags

We mentioned the various types of bags that can be used for sous vide cooking in the last chapter. The size of the food will determine the size of the bag used. Something like a roast or rack of ribs will require a much larger bag. Resealable plastic bags are perfectly good to use as long as you're cooking below 158°F. You can use mason jars for anything that will fit in them, but they're best used for foods that need to set like yogurt, custards, and pates.

How to Avoid Overcooking and Undercooking

The most important thing you can do to avoid overcooking or undercooking your food in your sous vide is to follow the instructions in the recipe. The recipes have been tested out so the temperature and timing work. Don't assume that cooking a piece of meat for a longer period of time will make it more tender. Overcooking in a sous vide will turn your food into mush. Eventually, the proteins break down too much, and the food loses its shape and texture. You also need to be careful when searing meat. If you sear meat for too long, it will overcook the meat.

Practice makes perfect, so the more you cook with it and experiment the better you'll get.

Can I Cook Something While I'm at Work?

You can cook larger things with extended cook times while you're at work. Anything that takes eight hours or more should be ok. The biggest problem you might run into is evaporation. You'll need a lid or some way of minimizing evaporation. You should test out a few longer cooks before trying it on a workday. That way you can relax and check your lid and water levels periodically.

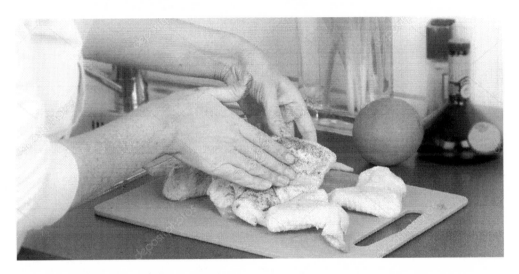

Guidelines on Marinating and Prepping Meats, Fish

It's important to realize that sous vide cooking intensifies flavors. Go light on seasoning especially salt. In most cases, a single sprig of fresh herbs will do. You want to go light on salt when doing long cooks because the salt could create a brine over time. When using butter or oil use just enough to coat the food. You don't want the food swimming in fat.

How to Keep Your Anova Clean

You can clean the various parts of your precision cooker easily. You can remove and place the end cap and the metallic housing in your dishwasher or clean it in the sink with a sponge and dish soap.

Over time your cooker can accumulate mineral deposits. Mix equal parts white vinegar and water in a small pot. Set up your cooker and set it to 140°F and allow the liquid to reach that temperature. When the cooker reaches 140°F, it's clean.

The insides of your cooker are best cleaned with a toothbrush and dish soap. Use a damp cloth to clean off the soap. The best way to keep it clean is to clean it every after use.

Use a damp microfiber cloth to clean the display. Then use a dry microfiber cloth to dry it off.

How to Store Your Sous Vide Leftovers

You can store your sous vide leftovers like many other leftovers. Make sure they're in an airtight container before placing them in the fridge. If you're using re-sealable silicone bags, make sure it's sealed properly and there's no excess air. When you're ready to eat your leftovers, you can sous vide them again for a short time to make sure they come out tasting delicious.

Using the Bluetooth App

The Anova app works via Bluetooth. You can use the app to control the device and monitor your food.

The iOS and Android apps can be downloaded at their respective stores and your device must have iOS 9.0 or Android 4.3 or later to function.

The app is designed for phone screens and will be slightly distorted if run on tablet devices.

To set it up, first enable Bluetooth then from inside the app hit 'Connect Anova' found on a blue bar towards the bottom of the screen.

Make sure the current temperature matches both the app and the display of the device. If it does not, tap 'no' and the app will search to reconnect again. If 'yes' then press the button and you will be connected to your device and returned to the homes screen which will show a green bar. You can remotely control your device from the app and find other recipes and save ones you like.

4

Pro Tips

Sear Meats for Better Texture and A Beautiful Appearance

Searing meat improves the texture of the exterior of the meat and adds a more complex flavor due to a chemical reaction call the Maillard reaction in which amino acids react with sugars to produce a distinctive charred flavor. There are some benefits to searing meat before placing it in your sous vide. It helps to break down the fat, which helps, in the cooking process. It also creates more flavors in the meat. That flavor gets intensified when it goes through the sous vide cooking process. If you decide to pre-sear your meat, make sure you put the seared meat in an unsealed bag, and then into an ice bath before placing it in your sous vide. Make sure the unsealed end is out of the water, so the meat doesn't get wet. The meat should stay in the ice bath for about 20 minutes. This step brings the food below room temperature. You want to do this so that you don't cook boiling juices in your sous vide. This could potentially destroy the meat.

Minimize Evaporation

It's important to minimize evaporation so that the water level doesn't get below the minimum line. This is especially important for longer cooking where there's a lot more evaporation. You can minimize evaporation using a few different methods depending on your container.

If your container has a lid, you may cut a hole in the lid that's big enough for your sous vide. Make sure you place aluminum foil on any open space surrounding the sous vide. Another good option is ping-pong balls. Yes, I said ping-pong balls. Cover the entire top of the container with ping-pong balls for an easy solution. The balls will stop the water from leaving the container and will keep your food from floating. Another option is plastic wrap. The two big drawbacks with this are that it can be tricky to use, and it punctures easily. Any holes will allow for evaporation to leak out.

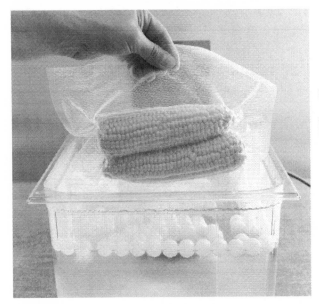

Fill Your Container with Ping Pong Balls to Minimize Evaporation.

Maximize Cooking Capacity

There's a couple of ways you can maximize your cooking capacity. You can place multiple bags into the container as long as they're not bumping up against each other. Delicate food like fish could lose its shape if it's continually bumping into other bags. You can also place multiple items in a single bag. Make sure the bag is not jam-packed. The food needs space to move around. If there's not enough space, the food might stick together and won't cook properly.

Plan Ahead

This might seem obvious, but it's important to plan ahead when using your sous vide. Many recipes require extended cooking times, some which can be up to 36 hours. Look over your recipe at least a day in advance so that you know how much time it will take. The last thing you want to do is go to the store to buy your ingredients after work and come home to realize the cooking process is going to take four hours.

Get the Air Out of Your Plastic Resealable Bag

There are a couple of different ways to get the air out of the resealable plastic bag. The first method is to close it up most of the way but leave about an inch of space. Put your lips up to that inch of space and suck as much air out as possible before closing it up.

Another sealing method is the submersion technique. Seal all but one corner of the bag and place it in water, allowing it to sink. As the bag submerges, the air will naturally be forced out. Right before the water reaches the top of the bag seal the corner of the bag before any water can get in.

Freeze Your Vacuum Seal Bags Before Use

It's a good idea to place your vacuum bag with food in the freezer for about 5 to 10 minutes before cooking. Part of what a vacuum sealer does is pull out moisture. If you put the bag in the freezer before sealing it, the juice in the food will set. If you have a high-end vacuum sealer it might come with a marinade or moisture control setting, which improves the vacuum sealing process for sous vide cooking.

Don't Over Vacuum Seal Your Fish

If you're using a vacuum sealer with fish or any other delicate food, it's important to make sure your vacuum sealer does not apply too much pressure to the fish. Too much pressure will cause the fish to lose its shape and some of its texture, and it may not come out as flaky as you'd like it to. You can prevent this by keeping close watch on your vacuum sealer as it seals and switch it from vacuuming to sealing just as all the air has been removed from the bag.

With Sous Vide There's No Need to Rest Meat

Generally, when cooking things like beef, you will need to rest it after cooking. Depending on how large a piece of meat you have, this time could range anywhere from ten minutes for an average steak, to about an hour for a rib roast. The reason meat needs to rest is to give the cooler internal temperature of the meat time to even out with the hotter external temperature of the surface of the meat. Allowing the meat to rest ensures that the juices within the meat will be fully absorbed and not lost when the meat is cut. When meat is cooked sous vide, this difference between the internal and external temperatures does not exist, which means meat cooked sous vide can be served right out of the bag. Or right out of the pan if you're searing it.

5

Beef Recipes

Boeuf Bourguignon

This delicious French dish is usually stewed, but stewing vegetables and meat together can leave the meat overcooked. Cooking the meat in your Anova Precision cooker ensures it's juicy and tender.

Servings: 3 | Prep Time: 25 Minutes | Cook Time: 24 Hours 40 Minutes

Ingredients

1 lb. stewing meat

salt and pepper to taste

2 sprigs fresh thyme

1 tablespoon of olive oil

1 medium sized onion finely chopped

2 garlic cloves finely chopped

3 slices smoky bacon cubed

1 cup button mushrooms cut into quarters

1 tablespoon butter

1 heaped tablespoon all-purpose flour

2 sprigs fresh thyme, stems removed

3/4 cups red wine

1 1/3 cups Beef stock

1/4 tsp. salt

freshly ground pepper

Directions

1. Preheat your Anova Precision Cooker to 140F or 60C.

2. While the Anova is preheating, cut the meat into cubes and remove the stems from the thyme leaves. Salt and pepper the meat to taste and season with the thyme. Seal the meat in your sous vide bag.

3. Place the bag in your preheated container and set your timer for 24 hours. Once cooked, open the pouch; save the juices and thyme from the pouch to use later.

4. Sear the meat in high heat with olive oil. Once seared, remove the meat. Add the onions to the skillet and cook for around 8 minutes, they should be golden and soft. Place the garlic and cook both for 2 minutes. Once cooked remove both from the skillet.

5.   Place the bacon in the skillet and cook for around 8 minutes. About halfway through the cooking add in the mushrooms. Once cooked, remove both from the skillet.

6.   Clean the skillet with a dry paper towel and then place it back on medium heat. Put in the butter and allow it to melt. Then, add in the flour and cook for around 5 minutes until the mixture is golden brown.

7.   Add the wine to the mixture and raise the heat to medium high. Stir frequently for a few minutes until the alcohol cooks off.

8.   Put in the beef stock, juices, and thyme leaves and allow the mixture to cook for 10 more minutes. The mixture will turn into a glossy and smooth sauce.

9.   Add in all the ingredients that you previously cooked in the skillet including the meat. Allow everything to cook for 8 minutes on medium heat. Add salt and pepper to taste.

10. Remove the mixture from the skillet and serve. It goes great with mashed potatoes.

Nutritional Info: Calories: 431, Sodium: 734 mg, Dietary Fiber: 2.2 g, Fat: 21.1 g, Carbs: 11.7 g, Protein: 36 g.

Rib-Eye Steak

The rib-eye is a tender cut of boneless meat with lovely fat marbling. This recipe adds aromatic herbs to compliment the lovely flavor of the meat.

Servings: 3 | Prep Time: 10 Minutes | Cook Time: 1 Hour

Ingredients

1 (16 - 18-ounce) boneless rib eye steak

Kosher salt and freshly ground black pepper, to taste

2 thyme sprigs

1 garlic clove

1 (4-inch) rosemary sprig

1 (3-inch) piece lemon zest

2 tbsp. vegetable oil

1 tablespoon unsalted butter

flaky sea salt, for garnish

Directions

1. Preheat your Anova Precision Cooker to 125F or 52C.

2. Season the meat with garlic, salt and pepper to taste.

3. Place the steak in your sous vide bag with the garlic, lemon zest, and herbs. Seal the bag and place it in your preheated container. Set the timer for 1 hour.

4. When the steak is cooked open the bag and pat the steak dry with a paper towel.

5. Heat a cast iron skillet over high heat and add the vegetable oil. Sear the steak for 1 to 2 minutes per side. Then quickly add in the butter and baste the steak with it for about 15 seconds.

6. Remove the steak from the skillet and let it rest for about 5 minutes before slicing it. Serve with garnish of flaked sea salt.

Nutritional Info: Calories: 469, Sodium: 187 mg, Dietary Fiber: 1.4 g, Fat: 30.2 g, Carbs: 3.6 g, Protein: 43.6 g.

Tender Brisket

This brisket will almost melt in your mouth it's so tender because it cooks low and slow allowing the connective tissue to completely break down. This succulent brisket makes the perfect center piece for a dinner party.

Servings: 8 | Prep Time: 15 Minutes | Cook Time: 72 Hours

Ingredients

4 lbs. beef brisket

1 tablespoon liquid smoke

1 tablespoon Worcestershire sauce

3 tsp. smoked paprika

1-1/2 tsp. garlic powder

1 tsp. onion powder

1/2 tsp. mustard powder

2 tsp. salt

1 tsp. pepper

Directions

1. Preheat your Anova Precision Cooker to 145F or 63C.

2. Mix together the liquid smoke and Worcestershire sauce in a bowl. Then, rub all over the brisket.

3. Combine the spices in a bowl with the salt and pepper. Rub the mixture on every part of the brisket.

4. Place the brisket in the sous vide bag and put in your preheated container. Set your Anova timer for 72 hours.

5. When the brisket is cooked, put on a grill that's set to medium high heat for 8-10 minutes. Turn the brisket often during grilling.

6. Serve the brisket with your favorite BBQ sauce.

Nutritional Info: Calories: 430, Sodium: 752 mg, Dietary Fiber: 0.5 g, Fat: 14.3 g, Carbs: 1.7 g, Protein: 69.1 g.

Corned Beef and Cabbage

This is the best corned beef you've ever had because it's so juicy and packed with flavor. The white wine and vinegar add a lovely depth to the cabbage while the long cooking time allows the beef to perfectly tenderize.

Servings: 8 | Prep Time: 20 Minutes | Cook Time: 48 Hours

Ingredients

4 lbs. brisket

2 tbsp. pickling spices

1 cup dark beef

1 cup beef stock

1 head of cabbage

1/4 cup white wine vinegar

6 strips of bacon

1 cup chicken stock

Directions

1. Preheat your Anova Precision Cooker to 135F or 57C. Rub the brisket with pickling spice.

2. Place the corned beef in the sous vide bag with the beer and stock and put it in your preheated container and cook for 48 hours.

3. Slice the cabbage into 1/2-inch wide pieces and cut the bacon into 1/4-inch pieces.

4. Remove the brisket from the bag and replace with chopped cabbage. Mix with the cooking liquid and seal the bag. Submerge in the water bath for 30 minutes

5. Place the bacon in a medium to large pan and cook it over medium heat until the fat is rendered.

6. The bacon should be nice and crispy. Remove all the bacon fat except for 1/4 tablespoon.

7. Remove the cabbage from the water bath and add to the pan, cooking for around 5 minutes.

8. Add in the vinegar and chicken stock and allow it to cook until the cabbage is tender.

9.   When the corned beef is done allow it to rest for about 5 minutes. Then cut it into equal portions. Serve the corned beef topped with cabbage.

Nutritional Info: Calories: 470, Sodium: 785 mg, Dietary Fiber: 2.2 g, Fat: 21.2 g,
Carbs: 6.4 g, Protein: 60 g.

Beef Tenderloin with Garlic and Port Wine

The tenderloin is an extremely lean and tender cut of meat. Cooking it with your Anova precision cooker ensures perfectly even results every time. The port and garlic give the meat an extraordinary depth of flavor.

Servings: 6 | Prep Time: 50 Minutes | Cook Time: 2 Hours 30 Minutes

Ingredients

2 lbs. center-cut beef tenderloin

1 tsp. salt

freshly ground black pepper

2 tbsp. vegetable oil divided

2 tbsp. butter

1/2 cup tawny port wine

4 to 5 medium cloves garlic

5 to 6 sprigs fresh thyme, plus extra to serve

Directions

1. Preheat your Anova Precision Cooker to 130F or 54C.

2. Cut the silver skin from the roast and tie it up with butcher's twine so it's uniform. Place the tenderloin in a sous vide bag and submerge in the water for 2 hours and 30 minutes.

3. Remove the tenderloin from the bag and salt and pepper the meat generously on all sides. Heat a skillet with 1 tablespoon of oil over high heat. Sear all sides of the roast, about 1 to 2 minutes per side.

4. Add the garlic and oil to the skillet and allow it to cook until the garlic becomes fragrant, about 60 seconds. Add the wine and deglaze using a spatula to scrape any brown chunks off of the skillet. Allow the wine to come to a simmer before taking the skillet off the heat.

5. Slice the tenderloin and serve with the pan jus.

6. Serve with your favorite side dish.

Nutritional Info: Calories: 314, Sodium: 474 mg, Dietary Fiber: 1 g, Fat: 19.7 g, Carbs: 3.7 g, Protein: 28.2 g.

Strip Steak with Rosemary and Thyme

The strip steak is a tender cut of meat with some fat marbling. The rosemary and thyme add a nice aromatic flavor to the meat.

Servings: 2 | Prep Time: 25 Minutes | Cook Time: 2 Hours 30 Minutes

Ingredients

1 (14-16 ounce) boneless strip steak (1 1/2-2-inch thick)

1/4 tsp. garlic powder

1/4 tsp. onion powder

1 tsp. kosher salt, plus more

1/4 tsp. freshly ground black pepper, plus more

3 sprigs rosemary

3 sprigs thyme

1 tablespoon grape seed or other neutral oil

Directions

1. Preheat your Anova Precision Cooker to 125F or 52C.

2. Season the steak with the garlic and onion powder, teaspoon of salt, and 1/4 tsp. of black pepper. Crush the rosemary and thyme on a cutting board to release the oils.

3. Place the steak in the sous vide bag with the rosemary and thyme.

4. Place the steak in your preheated container and set the Anova timer for 1 hour 30 minutes.

5. Remove the steak from the bag and heat the oil in a cast iron pan over high heat. Sear the steak on all sides for 1-2 minutes per side.

6. Serve whole or slice against the grain.

Nutritional Info: Calories: 650, Sodium: 203 mg, Dietary Fiber: 4.6 g, Fat: 26.6 g, Carbs: 8 g, Protein: 91.3 g.

Classic Meatballs

These meatballs make a great appetizer or the perfect filling for a meatball sandwich. Serve them plain or with the sauce of your choice.

Servings: 9 | Prep Time: 2 Hours 20 Minutes | Cook Time: 2 Hour

Ingredients

1 lb. ground beef (at least 85% lean)

1/2 lb. ground pork (or bulk ground sausage)

1 large egg

1/2 cup onion

1/2 cup Parmesan cheese

1/3 cup quick cooking oats

1/4 cup milk

3/4 tsp. salt

1/2 tsp. garlic powder

1/4 tsp. black pepper

Directions

1. Lightly beat the egg and finely chop the onion. Combine all ingredients until well mixed.

2. On a baking sheet, arrange the meatballs and place in the freezer for 1-2 hours.

3. Preheat your Anova Precision Cooker to 144F or 62C.

4. Place your steak into the sous vide bag and then the preheated container. Set your Anova timer for 2 hours 3 minutes.

5. Sear the meatballs for 1-2 minutes, flipping them halfway through.

6. Serve with your favorite sauce.

Nutritional Info: Calories: 161, Sodium: 267 mg, Dietary Fiber: 0.5 g, Fat: 5.3 g, Carbs: 3.2 g, Protein: 23.8 g.

Cheese Filled Hamburger

This hamburger has a melted cheesy surprise in the center. The burger comes out a perfect medium with a hot but not scorching melted cheese center. Add your favorite condiments to complete it.

Servings: 4 | Prep Time: 10 Minutes | Cook Time: 45 Minutes

Ingredients

---

24 oz. 80% meat 20% fat ground beef

Kosher salt to taste

4 slices American cheese

4 hamburger buns

condiments of your choice

1 tablespoon olive oil

Directions

---

1. Preheat your Anova Precision Cooker to 133F or 56C.

2. While your Anova is preheating, create 4 equal patties from the meat. Salt to taste.

3. Cut the cheese slices into 4 pieces. Stack the pieces in the middle of patties and form the meat over it.

4. Place the patties in a sous vide bag and put them in your preheated container. Set the Anova timer for 45 minutes.

5. Sear the meat on high heat. Serve with your favorite condiments.

Nutritional Info: Calories: 461, Sodium: 468 mg, Dietary Fiber: 0 g, Fat: 20.1 g, Carbs: 9.9 g, Protein: 57 g.

Carne Asada Tacos

These are the most tender and flavorful carne asada tacos you have ever tasted. Add your favorite taco condiments like avocado or onions for more flavors.

Servings: 4 | Prep Time: 8 Hours | Cook Time: 8 Hour

Ingredients

Skirt steak 1 1/2 lbs.

6 to 8 whole roasted green chilies

1 bunch of cilantro-about a cup (optional)

1/2 cup fresh lime juice

1/4 cup olive oil

1 1/2 tbsp. cumin powder (roasted)

3 cloves fresh garlic

1 tsp. ground oregano

1 tsp. salt

1 tablespoon whole black peppercorns

3 bay leaves

tortillas

Directions

1. Place the steak in the sous vide bag with the chilies and cilantro.

2. Mince the garlic and mix it with the remaining ingredients in a bowl.

3. Place the mixture in the bag with the steak. Allow it to marinate overnight in the refrigerator.

4. Preheat your Anova Precision Cooker to 132F or 55C. Take the garlic out of the bag.

5. Place your steak in the preheated contained and set your Anova timer for 8 hours. Once done, rest the steak for 5 minutes.

6. Keep the chilies and leftover juices for later.

7. Broil or grill the steak for 3-4 minutes each side to sear it. Allow the meat to rest for 5 more minutes.

8. Chop the meat into small pieces and sprinkle the leftover juices.

9. Serve with tortillas and the condiments of your choice.

Nutritional Info: Calories: 399, Sodium: 679 mg, Dietary Fiber: 2.6 g, Fat: 24.9 g,
Carbs: 13 g, Protein: 32.9 g.

Filet Mignon with Blue Cheese Sauce

Filet mignon is the most tender of all steaks. It doesn't have as much flavor as some of the fattier steaks, so the blue cheese sauce will provide added flavor.

Servings: 4 | Prep Time: 15 Minutes | Cook Time: 1 Hour

Ingredients

4 portions of filet mignon 1 inch thick, around 1-1/2 lbs.

salt and pepper

1 tablespoon garlic powder

2 tbsp. Worcester sauce

1/2 cup blue cheese

1/4 cup heavy cream

2 tbsp. lemon juice

3 tbsp. olive oil

lemon zest for garnish

Directions

1. Preheat your Anova Precision Cooker to 125F or 52C.

2. Season the steak with salt, pepper, and garlic powder. Place the steaks in the sous vide bag and add in the Worcester sauce.

3. Place the bag in your preheated container and set the Anova timer for 1 hour.

4. Combine the blue cheese, cream, lemon juice, and olive oil using a whisk or a blender. Salt and pepper to taste.

5. Once cooked, rest the steak for 5 minutes then top with blue cheese sauce.

6. Serve with a garnish of lemon zest on top.

Nutritional Info: Calories: 440, Sodium: 228 mg, Dietary Fiber: 0.1 g, Fat: 25.1 g, Carbs: 1.1 g, Protein: 50.1 g.

Wagyu Beef Cheeseburger

Wagyu is the king of all beef because of its amazing fat marbling and flavor. The Gruyère compliments the intense flavor the wagyu nicely.

Servings: 2 | Prep Time: 10 Minutes | Cook Time: 15 Minutes

Ingredients

2 (6-ounce) wagyu beef patties

Kosher salt and freshly ground black pepper

2 tbsp. extra-virgin olive oil

1 red onion

2 deli slices Gruyère cheese

2 burger buns

condiments and sauce of your choice

Directions

1. Preheat your Anova Precision Cooker to 143F or 62C. Chop the onions coarsely. Salt and pepper the patties to taste.

2. Place the patties in the sous vide bag and put them in your preheated container.

3. Place 1 tablespoon of olive oil in a skillet and heat it on medium heat. Once the olive oil is shimmering, put in the onions and allow them to cook for 5-7 minutes or until translucent.

4. Let the patties rest once cooked. Then turn your broiler on.

5. Sear the patties for 1 minute per side.

6. Put the patties on a broiler pan and place the cheese on top of the patties. Broil the patties until the cheese melts, around 1-3 minutes.

7. Place the patties on buns and serve with the onion and your favorite condiments.

Nutritional Info: Calories: 633, Sodium: 213 mg, Dietary Fiber: 2.7 g, Fat: 51.9 g, Carbs: 13.6 g, Protein: 28.3 g.

Pastrami

Perfectly juicy pastrami is easily made with your Anova Precision Cooker. The long cook time allows the meat to tenderize and absorb the rich spices.

Servings: 12 | Prep Time: 20 Minutes | Cook Time: 72 Hours

Ingredients

8-10 lbs. brisket

1-liter hot water

1-liter ice

100 grams kosher salt

20 grams caraway seeds

10 grams dill Seeds

50 grams coriander seeds

20 grams black pepper

10 grams allspice berries

5 grams clove

4 grams Lapsang Souchong tea or 5ml liquid smoke

4 bay leaves

Directions

1.   Mix together all of the ingredients except for the brisket in a large bowl. Cover it and refrigerate it overnight.

2.   Preheat your Anova Precision Cooker to 145 or 63C.

3.   Place the brisket in the sous vide bag with 1 cup of the brine.

4.   Place the brisket in your preheated container.

5.   When the pastrami is cooked allow it to rest for 5 minutes before cutting it in to slices.

6.   Serve anyway you would like.

Nutritional Info: Calories: 442, Sodium: 334 mg, Dietary Fiber: 1.9 g, Fat: 15.1 g, Carbs: 3.8 g, Protein: 69.6 g.

Flat Iron Steak with Red Wine Sauce

Flat iron is a fatty cut which benefits from the low, even heat of your Anova Precision Cooker. The red wine sauce perfectly complements the steak adding a delicious, rich flavor.

Servings: 4 | Prep Time: 20 Minutes | Cook Time: 2 Hours 30 Minutes

Ingredients

4 (8-16 ounce) flat iron
steaks

kosher salt and black pepper

8 small sprigs rosemary

1 tablespoon ghee

1/2 cup red wine

1 tablespoon cold butter

Directions

1. Preheat your Anova Precision Cooker to 128F or 53C. Season the steaks with salt and pepper to taste.

2. Place the steaks in a sous vide bag with a rosemary sprig for each steak. Place the steaks in your preheated container and set your Anova timer for 2 hours.

3. Once done, allow the steak to rest. Heat a skillet on high heat. When it's very hot, add in the ghee.

4. Sear the steak for about 1 minute per side. Remove the steaks and lower the temperature to medium high heat.

5. Add the wine to the skillet and cook until it reduces by half, stirring occasionally.

6. Slice the steaks against the grain while the sauce is cooking. Take the sauce off the heat when it's reduced the proper amount.

7. Mix in the cold butter, and salt to taste.

8. Pour the red wine sauce on top of the steak before serving.

Nutritional Info: Calories: 944, Sodium: 317 mg, Dietary Fiber: 2.8 g, Fat: 55.1 g, Carbs: 5 g, Protein: 94.4 g.

Top Sirloin Sandwich with Arugula

Top sirloin is typically a cheaper cut of meat, but it's made tender and flavorful in the sous vide. The balsamic, Dijon mustard, and goat cheese give the sandwich a complex flavor.

Servings: 4 | Prep Time: 20 Minutes | Cook Time: 2 Hours 5 Minutes

Ingredients

2 lbs. top sirloin cap roast

2 tsp. kosher salt

1 tsp. fresh ground black pepper

4 sprigs fresh thyme

4 cloves garlic

1 loaf crusty french bread

Arugula

Salt

Balsamic vinegar

Goat cheese

Dijon mustard

Directions

1. Preheat your Anova Precision Cooker to 125F or 52C.

2. Salt and pepper the roast with the kosher salt and ground pepper. Mince the garlic.

3. Place the roast in the sous vide bag with the thyme sprigs and garlic.

4. Place the steaks in your preheated container and set your Anova timer for 2 hours.

5. Preheat a grill to high heat. Slice the bread lengthwise first and then make another cut crosswise.

6. When the roast is done pat it dry with a paper towel and let it rest for 5 minutes.

7. Place the roast on the grill and grill it for 2 to 3 minutes per side. Remove the roast and place the bread on the grill for 30 seconds with the cut side down.

8. Cut the roast into thin slices and slice the bread.

9.   Spread the Dijon onto one slice of bread and spread goat cheese on the other. Add the slices of beef and top with arugula, salt, and a drizzle of balsamic vinegar.

Nutritional Info: Calories: 162, Sodium: 127 mg, Dietary Fiber: 1 g, Fat: 8.3 g, Carbs: 8.7 g, Protein: 12.6 g.

Hawaiian Style Short Ribs

These authentic Hawaiian short ribs become tender and flavorful because the connective tissue has a long time to break down while cooking in your Anova Precision cooker. The sweet BBQ sauce is exactly like the sauce you find in many restaurants throughout Hawaii.

Servings: 3 | Prep Time: 10 Minutes | Cook Time: 24 Hours

Ingredients

3/4 cups unsweetened pineapple juice

1/2 cup peanut oil

1/3 cup soy sauce

1/4 cup molasses

1 tsp. ground ginger

1 lb. short ribs

1 tsp. Kosher salt and freshly ground black pepper or more to taste

Directions

1. Combine everything except the ribs and salt and pepper in a bowl.

2. Place the ribs in a sous vide bag, add the sauce, and salt and pepper to taste. (go light on the salt)

3. Vacuum seal the bag and refrigerate overnight.

4. Preheat your Anova Precision Cooker to 155F or 68C.

5. Place the ribs in your preheated container and set your timer for 24 hours.

Nutritional Info: Calories: 1097, Sodium: 246 mg, Dietary Fiber: 0.4 g, Fat: 96.6 g, Carbs: 31 g, Protein: 25.7 g.

Taco Burgers

Everyone loves a traditional burger, but these unique sous vide burgers are infused with the flavor of classic tacos for a dish that will surprise and delight your friends and family.

Servings: 6 | Prep Time: 10 Minutes | Cook Time: 2 Hour 2 Minutes

Ingredients

1.5 lbs. ground beef

1 packet taco seasoning

2 eggs

12 slices cheddar cheese

6 hamburger buns

Salsa

sour cream

1 tablespoon olive oil

Directions

1. Preheat your Anova Precision Cooker to 130F or 54C.

2. Combine meat, taco seasoning, and egg in a bowl. Make 6 patties out of the mixture.

3. Place the patties in a sous vide bag. Then, place the bags in your preheated container and set your Anova timer for 2 hours.

4. Once cooked, allow the burgers to rest for 5 minutes. Meanwhile, heat the olive oil in a skillet on medium high heat. Sear the burgers for 2 minutes, flipping halfway through the process.

5. Serve on the bun topped with a layer of salsa and sour cream.

Nutritional Info: Calories: 607, Sodium: 159 mg, Dietary Fiber: 0.9 g, Fat: 31.3 g, Carbs: 24.1 g, Protein: 54.3 g.

6

Fish

Poached Tuna with Basil Butter

Sous viding the tuna in oil creates an amazingly soft texture. The basil butter gives the tuna a delicious fresh and aromatic flavor.

Servings: 2 | Prep Time: 15 Minutes | Cook Time: 26 Minutes

Ingredients

1 stick (1/2 cup) softened unsalted butter

1/3 cup fresh basil

2 cloves garlic

zest of 1 lemon

sea salt and freshly ground black pepper

2 7- ounce fresh tuna steaks, 1-inch thick

1-1 1/2cups extra virgin olive oil

sea salt and freshly ground black pepper

2 tablespoons vegetable oil

Directions

1. Preheat your Anova Precision Cooker to 110F or 43C. Finely mince the garlic and basil, and finely zest the lemon.

2. Mash together the butter with basil, garlic, and lemon zest until well mixed. Add salt and pepper to taste.

3. Put each piece of tuna in a separate sous vide bag and pour in 1/2-3/4 cups of oil in each bag.

4. Place the bag in your preheated container and set your timer for 25 minutes.

5. While the salmon is cooking, place the butter on one side of piece of plastic wrap.

6. Roll the butter in the plastic wrap to create a log. Place the butter in the refrigerator.

7. When the tuna is almost cooked, heat the vegetable oil in a skillet over high heat. Remove the tuna from the bag and sear for 30 seconds per side.

8.   Top with at least 1/2-inch-thick piece of basil butter to serve.

Nutritional Info: Calories: 746, Sodium: 50 mg, Dietary Fiber: 0.1 g, Fat: 61.6 g,
Carbs: 17.1 g, Protein: 30.3 g.

Clams with White Wine and Artichoke Hearts

This simple method for preparing clams with white wine guarantees the clams come out bursting with flavor while maintaining their delicate texture.

Servings: 4 | Prep Time: 30 Minutes | Cook Time: 11 Minutes

Ingredients

24 clams

1 cup marinated artichoke hearts

3 garlic cloves

2 tbsp. extra virgin olive oil

1 tablespoon cornstarch

1 cup veggie or fish stock

3 tbsp. white wine

salt and pepper to taste

parsley for garnish

Directions

1. Preheat your Anova Precision Cooker to 133F or 56C. Rinse the clams, slice the garlic, and cut the hearts in half.

2. Place stock and wine in a pot, heat until it boils. Place clams in boiling pot until they open. This should take around 1 minute.

3. Remove the clams from the pot and allow to cool for 15 minutes.

4. Place the cooled ingredients in a sous vide bag with the garlic and olive oil and place the bag in your preheated container for 3 minutes.

5. While the clams are cooking, heat a skillet over medium heat.

6. When the clams are cooked, transfer the liquid into the heated skillet. Mix in the corn starch until the sauce thickens.

7. Add in the artichoke heart until they're warm. Then mix in the clams for a few seconds before removing from heat.

8. Serve in bowls topped with parsley.

Nutritional Info: Calories: 158, Sodium: 217 mg, Dietary Fiber: 0.6 g, Fat: 10.3 g, Carbs: 5.5 g, Protein: 8.6 g.

Lime Shrimp with Cilantro Avocado Sauce

Fresh lime juice gives the shrimp a fresh citrus flavor, while the cilantro avocado sauce adds a floral creaminess which complements the bright, tangy citrus.

Servings: 4 | Prep Time: 10 Minutes | Cook Time: 15 Minutes

Ingredients

1 lb. shrimp, peeled and deveined

salt and pepper

2 tbsp. lime juice (juice of 2 limes)

3 tbsp. butter, cut into rough chunks

1/2 avocado, roughly diced

1/4 cup sour cream

1/2 tsp. kosher salt

Directions

1. Preheat your Anova Precision Cooker to 140F or 60C. Peel and devein the shrimp, dice the avocado roughly, and cut the butter into chunks.

2. Salt and pepper the shrimp to taste. Place it in the sous vide bag with the lime juice.

3. Place the bag in your preheated container and set your Anova timer for 15 minutes.

4. Meanwhile, place the avocado, sour cream, lime juice, and kosher salt in a blender or food processor, and blend until they become a smooth sauce.

5. Once the shrimp is cooked, top them with the sauce and serve.

Nutritional Info: Calories: 388, Sodium: 87 mg, Dietary Fiber: 1.8 g, Fat: 19 g, Carbs: 4.6 g, Protein: 48.5 g.

Salmon with Lemon and Dill

This delicate sous vide salmon pairs perfectly with the fresh flavors of lemon and dill for a dish balanced in flavor and texture.

Servings: 2 | Prep Time: 10 Minutes | Cook Time: 1 Hour 1 Hour

Ingredients

1 (1-lb) boneless salmon fillet

Kosher salt

1 tablespoon coarsely chopped dill

1 tsp. finely grated lemon zest

1/2 tsp. crushed red pepper flakes

1 tablespoon extra-virgin olive oil

1 tablespoon vegetable oil

Directions

1. Preheat your Anova Precision Cooker to 125F or 52C. Chop the dill coarsely and finely zest the lemon.

2. Salt the salmon to taste and mix the remaining spices in a bowl. Coat both sides of the salmon with the mixed herbs.

3. Place the salmon in the sous vide bag and add the oil before sealing.

4. Place the bag in your preheated container and set your timer for 1 hour.

5. Heat a skillet with the vegetable oil over medium high heat. Remove the salmon from the bag and sear, skin side down for 3 to 4 minutes. Serve crispy skin side up.

Nutritional Info: Calories: 366, Sodium: 103 mg, Dietary Fiber: 0.4 g, Fat: 21.2 g, Carbs: 1.3 g, Protein: 44.4 g.

Lobster Tail with Chimichurri Butter

Sous viding lobster ensures that it stays succulent and retains its robust flavor, and the chimichurri butter adds a burst of fresh citrus and herbs.

Servings: 2 | Prep Time: 10 Minutes | Cook Time: 35 Minutes

Ingredients

4 tbsp. softened unsalted butter

2 tbsp. parsley

2 tsp. fresh lemon juice

1 small garlic clove, finely minced

2 lobster tails, about 8 oz. each

1 lemon, halved

parsley for garnish

Directions

1. Preheat your Anova Precision Cooker to 135F or 57C. Chop the parsley, mince the garlic, and cut the lemon in half.

2. Mix the parsley, lemon juice, garlic, and butter in a bowl until well combined. Place the lobster in the sous vide bag with half of the butter and cook for 30 minutes.

3. When the lobster is almost finished cooking, preheat your grill so half the grill is on high heat and the other half is medium low.

4. When the lobster is cooked put them under cold water until cool and cut them in half lengthwise.

5. Place the tails on the hot side of the grill with the flesh side down for 2 minutes.

6. Flip the tails and baste with remaining butter, cooking another 2-3 minutes. Remove the tails from the grill. Allow the lemon pieces cook on the hot side of the grill with the flesh side down for 2-3 minutes.

7. Garnish the tails with parsley and serve with the grilled lemon.

Nutritional Info: Calories: 415, Sodium: 126 mg, Dietary Fiber: 0.6 g, Fat: 25 g, Carbs: 2.2 g, Protein: 43.7 g.

Lobster Ttail in Butter with Tarragon

The lobster is so flavorful thanks to the butter infused with tarragon. And best of all, it's quick and easy to prepare.

Servings: 2 | Prep Time: 10 Minutes | Cook Time: 30 Minutes

Ingredients

pinch of salt and pepper

8 tbsp. of butter

sprig of tarragon

2 lobster tails, about 8 oz. each

2 lemon wedges

Directions

1. Preheat your Anova Precision Cooker to 135F or 57C. Bring a pot of water to a boil.

2. Place the lobster in the boiling water for 1 minute. Make a cut in the lobster shell lengthwise.

3. Put the tails in the bag of your choice with 6 tbsp. of butter and tarragon and place the bag in your preheated container and set your timer for 30 minutes.

4. When the lobster is almost done cooking, melt the remaining butter in a pan on medium heat.

5. Serve the lobster with a side of melted butter and lemon wedges.

Nutritional Info: Calories: 461, Sodium: 603` mg, Dietary Fiber: 0.2 g, Fat: 46.6 g, Carbs: 0.8 g, Protein: 11.4 g.

Scallops with Brown Butter

Scallops are delicious but very delicate and can end up rubbery. Sous viding the scallops keeps their delicate texture intact. The brown butter infuses a delicious nutty, caramel flavor.

Servings: 2 | Prep Time: 5 Minutes | Cook Time: 35 Minutes

Ingredients

8.5 oz. scallops   salt & pepper

4 tsp. brown butter

Directions

1. Preheat your Anova Precision Cooker to 140F or 60C. Use a paper towel to gently dry the scallops.

2. Place the scallops in the sous vide bag with 2 tsp. of brown butter and salt and pepper to taste.

3. Place the bag or bags in your preheated container and set your Anova timer to 35 minutes.

4. Heat the remaining brown butter in a skillet on high heat.

5. When the scallops are cooked, take them out of the bag and place them in the skillet. Sear them for 30 seconds a side. They should have a golden color on both sides when seared.

Nutritional Info: Calories: 208, Sodium: 196 mg, Dietary Fiber: 0 g, Fat: 12.4 g, Carbs: 2.9 g, Protein: 20.3 g.

Charred Calamari with Miso and Mirin

This calamari comes out crunchy on the outside, but tender and delicious on the inside. The marinade provides a lovely subtle umami flavor.

Servings: 2 | Prep Time: 15 Minutes | Cook Time: 2 Hours 20 Minutes

Ingredients

2 tbsp. cooking sake

2 tbsp. miso paste

2 tbsp. mirin

2 tbsp. light brown sugar

3 tbsp. chili oil

8 oz. squid bodies

1 medium lemon

Directions

1. Preheat your Anova Precision Cooker to 138F or 59C. Clean and cut the calamari into thin rings and juice the lemon.

2. Mix the sake, sugar, miso, and mirin in a bowl. Add in the calamari and toss until well coated. Place the calamari and marinade in the sous vide bag and cook for 2 hours.

3. In the last couple minutes of cooking, heat a grill pan on high heat.

4. When the calamari is cooked, gently pat it dry using a paper towel. Sear the calamari in batches for 30 seconds. Place seared calamari in a bowl. Mix in the lemon juice and the chili oil.

5. Serve immediately.

Nutritional Info: Calories: 438, Sodium: 774 mg, Dietary Fiber: 1.7 g, Fat: 23.2 g, Carbs: 24.2 g, Protein: 19.1 g.

Cajun Spiced Tilapia

This recipe has all the spicy Cajun flavor you would find in Louisiana and it's a quick and easy recipe that's ready in under an hour.

Servings: 4 | Prep Time: 10 Minutes | Cook Time: 30 Minutes

Ingredients

4 tilapia fillets

1 tablespoon black pepper

1 tablespoon kosher salt

1 tablespoon smoked paprika

2 tbsp. Italian seasoning

2 tbsp. cayenne pepper

2 tbsp. garlic powder

2 tbsp. dried onion granules or onion powder

1 tablespoon vegetable oil

Directions

1. Preheat your Anova Precision Cooker to 138F or 59C. Pat the fish dry using a paper towel.

2. Mix together all the spices in a bowl and rub the spice mixture on the fish.

3. Place the fish in the sous vide bag and cook for 30 minutes.

4. Heat the oil in a skillet over medium high heat and add the fish to the pan searing for 1 minute per side.

Nutritional Info: Calories: 188, Sodium: 179 mg, Dietary Fiber: 2.4 g, Fat: 7.3 g, Carbs: 10.1 g, Protein: 22.9 g.

Swordfish with Balsamic Brown Butter Sauce

This swordfish comes out so tender and melt in your mouth good and the sauce adds a nutty, sweet flavor to the fish.

Servings: 4 | Prep Time: 20 Minutes | Cook Time: 30 Minutes

Ingredients

2 lbs. swordfish steaks

salt and pepper

zest from 1/2 lemon

1 stick unsalted butter

3 tbsp. balsamic vinegar

3 tbsp. honey

1 tablespoon Dijon mustard

Directions

1. Preheat your Anova Precision Cooker to 126F or 52C.

2. Salt and pepper your steaks to taste and season with lemon zest.

3. Place the steaks in the sous vide bag and place in the water bath for 30 minutes.

4. Add the butter in a saucepan over medium heat until it foams. Once it stops foaming and turns a golden brown, whisk in the balsamic vinegar, Dijon and honey. Lower the heat to a simmer and allow the sauce to thicken.

5. Remove the steaks from the bag and top with the sauce to serve.

Nutritional Info: Calories: 634, Sodium: 446 mg, Dietary Fiber: 0.2 g, Fat: 34.5 g, Carbs: 15.3 g, Protein: 64.3 g.

Cod with Lemon and Capers

This simple recipe teaches you how to make cod which is moist and delicious. The lemon and capers highlight the delicate flavor of the fish.

Servings: 2 | Prep Time: 10 Minutes | Cook Time: 30 Minutes

Ingredients

2 (6-ounce) cod fillets

salt and freshly ground black pepper

1/2 lemon sliced into 4 rounds

1/4 cup plus 1 tablespoon extra-virgin olive oil

12 tsp. capers

fresh dill

Directions

1. Preheat your Anova Precision Cooker to 120F or 49C. Slice the lemon into four pieces and chop the dill.

2. Salt and pepper the cod to taste. Place the cod in the sous vide bag and add 2 pieces of lemon. Pour in 1/4 cup of oil and the capers.

3. Place your bag in the preheated container and set your timer for 30 minutes.

4. When the cod is done, top with olive oil and the dill.

Nutritional Info: Calories: 265, Sodium: 61 mg, Dietary Fiber: 0.9 g, Fat: 15.7 g, Carbs: 2.1 g, Protein: 30.9 g.

Halibut with Rosemary and Kaffir Lime Leaves

The halibut is poached in milk, which helps to it stay moist and adds creaminess. The kaffir lime leaves add a delicious southeast Asian flavor.

Servings: 4 | Prep Time: 15 Minutes | Cook Time: 15 Minutes

Ingredients

4 halibut fillets, each 6 oz. and 1 1/2 inches-thick

Kosher salt

1/2 cup milk

3 fresh rosemary sprigs

4 kaffir lime leaves

Directions

1. Preheat your Anova Precision Cooker to 125F or 52C. Slice the lime leaves thinly.

2. Salt the halibut and place it in the sous vide bag with the remaining ingredients.

3. Place the bag in your preheated container and set your Anova timer for 15 minutes. Remove and serve immediately.

Nutritional Info: Calories: 214, Sodium: 106 mg, Dietary Fiber: 1.1 g, Fat: 5 g, Carbs: 3.1 g, Protein: 37.1 g.

Red Snapper with Fennel Seeds and Chili Flakes

This is an easy recipe that doesn't require much time and the chili flakes add some heats to this flavorful fish while the fennel adds a subtle licorice flavor.

Servings: 2 | Prep Time: 15 Minutes | Cook Time: 25 Minutes

Ingredients

---

1 lb. red snapper (skinned, pin bones removed, and portioned)

3 tbsp. of salted butter

1.5 tbsp. fennel seeds

1 tsp. chili flakes

1 tablespoon kosher salt

1/2 lemon

Directions

---

1. Preheat your Anova Precision Cooker to 131F or 55C. Use a paper towel to pat the snapper dry. Juice the lemon.

2. Use mortar and pestle or a spice grinder to combine the chili, salt, and fennel sides. Season the snapper with the spice mixture.

3. Place the snapper in the sous vide bag with half the butter, and place in the water bath for 25 minutes.

4. When the snapper is done, put the juices from the bag in a saucepan over medium heat while adding in the butter and lemon juice. Whisk until the sauce comes together, around 3 minutes.

5. Serve the snapper with the sauce on top.

Nutritional Info: Calories: 462, Sodium: 313 mg, Dietary Fiber: 2.2 g, Fat: 21.9 g, Carbs: 3.7 g, Protein: 60.7 g.

Brined Salmon

This recipe is simple and allows you to taste the delicious flavor of the salmon. Brining the salmon helps it to maintain its moisture while improving flavor and texture.

Servings: 4 | Prep Time: 5 Hours 15 Minutes | Cook Time: 25 Minutes

Ingredients

4 salmon fillets

6 tbsp. unsalted butter

3 tbsp. sugar

fresh ground pepper

5 tablespoons coarse salt, plus more for taste

1/2 cup olive oil or melted, cooled butter

Directions

1. Place 4 1/2 cups of water in a large bowl. Pour in the 5 tbsp. of salt and 3 tbsp. of sugar. Stir the mixture until all solids dissolve. Place the salmon in the mixture and submerge. Place the bowl in the refrigerator for 5 hours.

2. Preheat your Anova Precision Cooker to 115F or 46C. Take the salmon out of the bowl and place it in separate Sous vide bags along with 2 tbsp. of olive oil.

3. Place the bags in your preheated container and set your Anova timer for 24 minutes.

4. In the last few minutes of cooking, place the 6 tbsp. of butter in a skillet and melt it over medium low heat.

5. When the salmon is cooked, salt and pepper to taste. Place the salmon in the skillet and allow it to cook for 30 seconds per side. Serve immediately.

Nutritional Info: Calories: 399, Sodium: 876 mg, Dietary Fiber: 0 g, Fat: 28.8 g, Carbs: 9 g, Protein: 24 g.

King Crab Legs with Herbed Butter

Sous vide crab legs retain so much moisture because they never touch boiling water and the herbed butter adds an aromatic decadence to the rich flavor of the crab.

Servings: 4 | Prep Time: 25 Minutes | Cook Time: 45 Minutes

Ingredients

2 lbs. king crab legs

8 tbsp. unsalted butter

2 tsp. grated lemon zest

4 tsp. parsley

2 tsp. thyme

2 garlic cloves

1/2 tsp. salt

freshly ground black pepper

Directions

1. Preheat your Anova Precision Cooker to 115F or 46C.

2. Finely chop the parsley and thyme, soften the butter, and peel and finely chop the garlic. Mix together all the ingredients except for the crab. Allow it to rest for 15 minutes.

3. Carefully cut open one side of the crab legs to expose the flesh. Pack the exposed side with the herbed butter. Place the remaining butter in the refrigerator and put the legs in the sous vide bag. You may need to double bag them to avoid punctures.

4. Place the bag in your preheated container and set your timer for 45 minutes.

5. When the legs are cooked place any leftover juice in a serving container with the remaining herbed butter.

6. Serve the legs with the butter on the side for dipping.

Nutritional Info: Calories: 205, Sodium: 141 mg, Dietary Fiber: 0.3 g, Fat: 13 g, Carbs: 1.1 g, Protein: 20.2 g.

East Asian Marinated Catfish

This dish is so full of flavor you think it's from an authentic Chinese restaurant. It's bursting with deep umami flavors and just the right amount of heat.

Servings: 4 | Prep Time: 10 Minutes | Cook Time: 20 Minutes

Ingredients

4 catfish filets

1/3 cup vegetable oil

1/4 cup low sodium soy sauce

2 cloves garlic minced

2 tbsp. rice wine vinegar

2 tbsp. sesame seeds

1 tablespoon sesame oil

1/4 tsp. black pepper

1/4 tsp. red pepper flakes

Directions

1. Preheat your Anova Precision Cooker to 150F or 66C.

2. Combine all the ingredients in a bowl except for the catfish. Place the catfish in a bag and pour the mixture in.

3. Place the bag or bags in your preheated container and set your timer for 20 minutes.

4. When the catfish is cooked, serve it with the leftover sauce in the bag.

Nutritional Info: Calories: 463, Sodium: 142 mg, Dietary Fiber: 2.8 g, Fat: 38.3 g, Carbs: 7.1 g, Protein: 23.7 g.

Spanish Spiced Shrimp

This dish is packed with authentic flavors of Spain. The paprika gives it a nice smoky flavor, while the sherry adds sweetness.

Servings: 3 | Prep Time: 15 Minutes | Cook Time: 20 Minutes

Ingredients

1 1/2 lbs. shrimp

kosher salt and pepper

2 tbsp. olive oil

6 garlic cloves

1 tablespoon Spanish hot smoked paprika

1 tablespoon sweet smoked paprika

4 tbsp. sherry

2 tbsp. butter

6 lemon wedges

Directions

1. Preheat your Anova Precision Cooker to 120F or 49C. Peel and devein the shrimp and mince the garlic. Salt and pepper the shrimp to taste.

2. Put the olive oil in a skillet and heat it over medium low heat. Add the garlic and paprika and allow it to cook for 2-3 minutes.

3. Add the sherry and raise the temperature to high, cooking for 2-3 minutes. Remove from the heat and mix in the butter and add salt. Allow the sauce to cool for 15 minutes.

4. Place the shrimp in the sous vide bag and pour in the sauce and cook for 20 minutes.

5. Serve the shrimp with the lemon wedges.

Nutritional Info: Calories: 456, Sodium: 610 mg, Dietary Fiber: 8.2 g, Fat: 21.2 g, Carbs: 8.2 g, Protein: 52.6 g.

7

Poultry Recipes

Molten Teriyaki Chicken

This chicken has an amazing caramelized taste because it is quickly seared in the broiler. Cooking sous vide ensures your chicken is always tender.

Servings: 2 | Prep Time: 15 Minutes | Cook Time: 45 Minutes

Ingredients

2 skinless boneless chicken breasts

1 tsp. ginger juice

2 tsp. unrefined sugar

1 tsp. salt

4 tbsp. unrefined sugar

4 tbsp. soy sauce

4 tbsp. sake

Directions

1. Preheat your Anova Precision Cooker to 145F or 63C.

2. Cover the chicken with the ginger juice. Combine the salt and sugar in a small bowl. Season the chicken with it.

3. Place the chicken in the sous vide bag and cook for 45 minutes.

4. Preheat the broiler and pat the chicken dry using a paper towel, and coat with sauce.

5. Place the remaining ingredients on a broiler rack and cook until it bubbles and becomes thick.

6. Slice the chicken into pieces and top with the remaining sauce to serve.

Nutritional Info: Calories: 176, Sodium: 304 mg, Dietary Fiber: 0.4 g, Fat: 1.6 g, Carbs: 8.1 g, Protein: 28.1 g.

Crispy Thyme Chicken Thighs

This chicken has delicious crispy skin, which gives it a nice crunch. The thyme adds a lovely aromatic flavor, which is balanced nicely by the umami of the fish sauces.

Servings: 4 | Prep Time: 15 Minutes | Cook Time: 3 Hours

Ingredients

4 pieces free-range chicken thighs, skin on, bone in

8 sprigs fresh thyme

2 tbsp. butter cut into 4 pieces

grated zest of 1 lemon

1 tablespoon fish sauce

Kosher salt

fresh cracked black pepper

1/4 cup olive oil

Directions

1. Preheat your Anova Precision Cooker to 150F or 65C.

2. Put the thighs in the sous vide bag with salt, pepper, butter, thyme, fish sauce, and lemon zest.

3. Place the bag in your preheated container and set your Anova timer for 3 hours. Allow the chicken to rest for 10 minutes.

4. Heat the oil in a skillet over medium-low heat. Place the rested chicken in the skillet, skin side down. Cook for 7-10 minutes or until crispy. Flip the thighs over and allow them to cook for another 3-4 minutes.

5. Remove the chicken from the pan and boil the remaining juices on high heat and allow to reduce by half. Mix in 1/2 tablespoon of butter and the juice from half the lemon. Remove the pan from the heat.

6. Serve the chicken topped with the sauce.

Nutritional Info: Calories: 310, Sodium: 436 mg, Dietary Fiber: 3.8 g, Fat: 27.6 g, Carbs: 7.6 g, Protein: 11.3 g.

Honey Garlic Chicken Wings

These wings have a nice balance of sweet and savory thanks to garlic and honey. The wings turn out crunchy on the outside, but oh so tender on the inside.

Servings: 4 | Prep Time: 10 Minutes | Cook Time: 4 Hours 15 Minutes

Ingredients

40 chicken wings

12 cloves of garlic

2-inch nub of ginger

8 tbsp. of honey

4 tbsp. of soy sauce

salt and pepper

Directions

1. Preheat your Anova Precision Cooker to 160F or 71C. Chop the garlic and the ginger.

2. Mix together all the ingredients in a bowl. Add salt and pepper to taste. Reserve 4 tablespoons of the mixture for later use.

3. Place the wings and the sauce in a sous vide bag, and coat with the sauce.

4. Place the bag in your preheated container and set your Anova timer for 4 hours.

5. When the wings are almost cooked, preheat your broiler to 500F. Use parchment paper to line a rimmed baking sheet.

6. When the wings are cooked, put them on the baking sheet and place them under the broiler. Allow them to cook for 10-15 seconds. Flip the wings about halfway through the broiling process.

7. Toss broiled wings with the reserved sauce and serve immediately.

Nutritional Info: Calories: 155, Sodium: 91 mg, Dietary Fiber: 39.1 g, Fat: 0.4 g, Carbs: 39.1 g, Protein: 2 g.

Super Spicy Habanero Chicken Wings

These wings are incredibly spicy thanks to the habanero but use caution when handling the habaneros because their oil can burn and stays around unless wiped off well.

Servings: 4 | Prep Time: 10 Minutes | Cook Time: 4 Hours 15 Minutes

Ingredients

40 chicken wings

24 habanero peppers

4 tsp. oil or butter

12 tbsp. white vinegar

Directions

1. Preheat your Anova Precision Cooker to 160F or 71C. Chop the garlic and the ginger.

2. Place all the ingredients into a food processor or blender and blend until smooth. Reserve 4 tablespoons of the mixture for later use.

3. Place the wings and the sauce in a sous vide bag, and coat with the sauce.

4. Place the bag in the preheated container and set your Anova timer for 4 hours.

5. When the wings are almost cooked, preheat your broiler to 500F. Use parchment paper to line a rimmed baking sheet.

6. When the wings are cooked, put them on the baking sheet and place them under the broiler. Allow them to cook for 10-15 seconds. Flip the wings about halfway through the broiling process.

7. Toss the broiled wings with the reserved sauce and serve immediately.

Nutritional Info: Calories: 199, Sodium: 66 mg, Dietary Fiber: 4.1 g, Fat: 8.4 g, Carbs: 25.6 g, Protein: 7.5 g.

New York Butter Chicken Wings

Classic Buffalo wings are the perfect party snack, and these wings have just the right texture and heat.

Servings: 4 | Prep Time: 10 Minutes | Cook Time: 4 Hours 15 Minutes

Ingredients

40 chicken wings

8 tbsp. hot sauce

4 tablespoons butter

Salt and pepper

Directions

1. Preheat your Anova Precision Cooker to 160F or 71C.

2. Mix together all the ingredients in a bowl. Add salt and pepper. Reserve 4 tablespoons of the mixture for later use.

3. Place the wings and the sauce in a bag, and coat with the sauce.

4. Place the sous vide bag in your preheated container and cook for 4 hours.

5. When the wings are almost cooked, preheat your broiler to 500F. Use parchment paper to line a rimmed baking sheet.

6. When the wings are cooked, put them on the baking sheet and place them under the broiler. Allow them to cook for 10-15. Flip the wings about halfway through the broiling process.

7. Toss broiled wings with the reserved sauce and serve immediately.

Nutritional Info: Calories: 145, Sodium: 88 mg, Dietary Fiber: 0.1 g, Fat: 14.3 g, Carbs: 1.9 g, Protein: 2.7 g.

Balsamic and Honey Duck Breast

Duck has a rich flavor on its own. The honey and balsamic give this duck a sweet and tangy flavor that matches the richness of the duck well.

Servings: 2 | Prep Time: 20 Minutes | Cook Time: 1 Hour 5 Minutes

Ingredients

2 duck breast

2 sprigs thyme leaves

sea salt and black pepper

3 tablespoons balsamic vinegar

1 1/2 tablespoons honey

Directions

1. Preheat your Anova Precision Cooker to 135F or 57C. Score the skin side of the breast.

2. Salt and pepper the duck and place it in a sous vide bag. Place a sprig of thyme on each breast and cook for 2 hours.

3. Heat a pan on medium high heat. When the duck is cooked, place it skin side down in the pan. Allow the skin side to cook for about 5 minutes or until it turns golden. Flip the breasts over and cook an additional 30 seconds. Remove the duck from the pan and let it rest for 5 minutes.

4. Pour the duck fat out of the pan and pour in the balsamic vinegar. Allow the balsamic to come to a boil and cook until it thickens. Mix in the honey and allow it to boil. Remove from the heat and salt and pepper to taste.

5. Serve the duck sliced topped with the sauce.

Nutritional Info: Calories: 271, Sodium: 4 mg, Dietary Fiber: 1.6 g, Fat: 6.7 g, Carbs: 15.9 g, Protein: 35.6 g.

Spicy Fried Chicken

This fried chicken is perfectly crunchy on the outside and perfectly tender and juicy on the inside. The addition of hot sauce gives it just the right amount of heat.

Servings: 3 | Prep Time: 20 Minutes | Cook Time: 2 Hours 10 Minutes

Ingredients

6 whole chicken drumsticks

2 eggs

2 tbsp. hot sauce (optional)

Marinade:

1 tablespoon kosher salt

1 tsp. ground black pepper

1 tsp. garlic powder

1/2 tsp. smoked paprika

1/4 tsp. cayenne

Spices mix:

2 cups all-purpose flour

1/4 cup cornstarch

1 tsp. kosher salt

1 tsp. ground black pepper

1 tsp. garlic powder

1/2 tsp. smoked paprika

5 cups canola oil

Directions

1. Preheat your Anova Precision Cooker to 155F or 68C.

2. Mix the marinade mixture using a whisk. Season the chicken with the mixture. Place the chicken in the sous vide bag and cook for 2 hours.

3. Place the bag in your preheated container and set your Anova timer for 2 hours.

4. Beat the egg in a medium size bowl and mix in the hot sauce. In large resealable plastic bag, add in spices and mix together.

5. When the chicken is cooked, pour the oil into the cast iron skillet and heat it to 350F. Take the chicken out of the bag and coat it with the egg mixture.

6. Place 2 drumsticks in the zip-lock bag that contain the spices, seal it, and shake it until the chicken is coated.

7. Fry the drumsticks in the pot or skillet, for about 2 minutes a side or until golden brown. Place them on a paper towel lined dish when finished. Use another paper towel to pat the chicken and remove excess oil.

8. Serve immediately.

Nutritional Info: Calories: 403, Sodium: 265 mg, Dietary Fiber: 1.3 g, Fat: 31.2 g, Carbs: 20.2 g, Protein: 12.7 g.

Duck Breast with Amarena Cherry Sauce

This duck breast combines rich cherries and wine for a rich flavor that is sure to please your guests.

Servings: 4 | Prep Time: 15 Minutes | Cook Time: 1 Hour

Ingredients

4 duck breasts

1 small jar of amarena cherries in syrup

1 cup red wine

4 sprigs of thyme

5 tbsp. butter

Directions

1. Preheat your Anova Precision Cooker to 145F or 63C. Wash and dry the duck, and then cut the skin off of it. Salt and pepper the duck to taste. Place the duck in the sous vide bag with 1 tablespoon of butter and 1 sprig of thyme on each breast.

2. Place in the preheated container & set timer for 1 hour.

3. Place cherries and wine in a pan and bring to a boil over high heat.

4. Reduce the temperature to medium heat and cook until the sauce becomes thick. Take the pan off the heat.

5. When the duck is cooked, pat it dry and heat a skillet on medium heat with a tablespoon of butter.

6. Once the skillet is hot, add in the duck and sear it for about a minute per side.

7. Serve topped with the cherry sauce.

Nutritional Info: Calories: 373, Sodium: 104 mg, Dietary Fiber: 0.5 g, Fat: 20.9 g, Carbs: 4.7 g, Protein: 35.5 g.

Duck Leg Confit

This process allows the fat in the duck to render resulting in the most tender and richly flavored duck you've ever had.

Servings: 2 | Prep Time: 6 Hours 10 Minutes | Cook Time: 8 Hours 2 Minutes

Ingredients

2 duck breasts

100 grams salt

bay leaf

sprig of thyme

2 thin orange slices

1 clove garlic

salt and pepper

2 tbsp. duck fat or olive oil

Directions

1. Place all the ingredients in a medium size bowl and mix until the salt dissolves. Place the duck in the bowl and refrigerate for 6 hours covered.

2. Preheat your Anova Precision Cooker to 176F or 80C.

3. Take the duck out of the mixture and pat it dry using a paper towel. Salt and pepper the duck to taste and place it in the sous vide bag with the oil or fat.

4. Place the bag or your preheated container and set your Anova timer for 8 hours.

5. When the duck is almost done cooking, preheat your broil to high.

6. When the duck is done cooking, broil it until skin side becomes crispy.

Nutritional Info: Calories: 351, Sodium: 193 mg, Dietary Fiber: 1.2 g, Fat: 20.5 g, Carbs: 6.1 g, Protein: 35.8 g.

Turkey Breast with Rosemary Orange Butter

The turkey comes out juicy with delicious, crunchy skin. The rosemary orange butter adds a sweet and savory flavor.

Servings: 6 | Prep Time: 15 Minutes | Cook Time: 1 Hour 35 Minutes

Ingredients

2 boneless turkey breast halves with skin

1/4 unsalted butter

1 tablespoon honey

1 tsp. fresh rosemary

zest of 1 navel orange

1/2 tsp. salt

1/8 tsp. ground black pepper

1/8 tsp. crushed red pepper

1 1/2 tsp. kosher salt

2 sprigs fresh rosemary

Directions

1. Preheat your Anova Precision Cooker to 150F or 66C. Chop the rosemary and soften the butter.

2. Combine butter, honey, chopped rosemary, orange zest, and 1/2 tsp. of salt in a bowl. Remove skin from one side of each breast half. Season turkey with kosher salt, black pepper, and crushed red pepper. Place butter mixture under the skin of the turkey and rub on top of skin.

3. Place the turkey in bags and put 1 sprig of rosemary in each bag.

4. Place the bags in your preheated container and set your Anova timer for 1 hour 30 minutes.

5. Towards the end of the cooking process, preheat your broiler on high.

6. When the turkey is cooked, put it under the broiler with the skin side up until the skin gets crispy, about 5 minutes.

7. Slice the turkey and serve immediately.

Nutritional Info: Calories: 43, Sodium: 34 mg, Dietary Fiber: 1.4 g, Fat: 0.6 g, Carbs: 7.2 g, Protein: 2.6 g.

Lemon Herb Turkey Breast

This dish requires very little prep on your part but is full of flavor. The lemon adds a tangy citrus flavor that pairs well with the flavor of the fresh herbs.

Servings: 2 | Prep Time: 5 Minutes | Cook Time: 4 Hours

Ingredients

2 lbs. boneless, skinless turkey breast

1/4 cup honey

1/4 cup lemon juice

1 tsp. dried dill or 1 tablespoon fresh

1 tsp. dried parsley or 1 tablespoon fresh

1 tsp. dried basil or 1 tablespoon fresh

1/4 tsp. black pepper

1 tsp. salt

2 tbsp. flour

Directions

1. Preheat your Anova Precision Cooker to 143F or 62C.

2. Combine all the ingredients except for the turkey and flour in a bowl. Place the turkey in the sous vide bag along with the marinade mixture and cook for 4 hours

3. When the turkey is cooked, put the flour in a small saucepan along with 1 tablespoon of oil. Heat the mixture over medium heat, stirring constantly for about 1 minute. Pour in the juices from the bag and use a whisk to remove any lumps from the gravy.

4. Slice the turkey thin and serve with the gravy.

Nutritional Info: Calories: 639, Sodium: 577 mg, Dietary Fiber: 2.9 g, Fat: 7.9 g, Carbs: 61.9 g, Protein: 78.8 g.

Tagliatelle with Turkey Thighs

This dish has only 4 ingredients, but it is still packed with flavor. It takes 24 hours for the turkey to cook, but the accumulated juices make an excellent sauce.

Servings: 2 | Prep Time: 5 Minutes | Cook Time: 24 Hours

Ingredients

2/3 lb. boneless, skinless turkey thigh

1/3 lb. dry tagliatelle

salt and fresh ground pepper

Directions

1. Preheat your Anova Precision Cooker to 165F or 74C.

2. Salt and pepper the turkey to taste and place it in the sous vide.

3. Place the bag in your preheated container and set your Anova timer for 24 hours.

4. Boil a large pot of salter water.

5. When pasta is just about ready, heat the juice on high heat until they boil. Turn the heat down to low. Mix in the shredded turkey and then the pasta when it's ready.

Nutritional Info: Calories: 571, Sodium: 240 mg, Dietary Fiber: 1.5 g, Fat: 9 g, Carbs: 39.8 g, Protein: 77.3 g.

Turkey Drumsticks with Rosemary and Sage

These turkey drumsticks make a great meal with a vegetable or other side. The turkey is full of flavor which is heightened by the sage and rosemary.

Servings: 2 | Prep Time: 15 Minutes | Cook Time: 8 Hours

Ingredients

2 (1-lb.) turkey legs

3 tbsp. butter

4 whole large fresh sage leaves

1 large sprig rosemary

2 cloves of garlic peeled

1/2 tsp. salt

1/2 tsp. freshly-ground black pepper

Directions

1. Preheat your Anova Precision Cooker to 165F or 74C. Crush the sage and smash the garlic.

2. Use a paper towel to pat dry the turkey, and place in the sous vide bag with the other ingredients.

3. Place the bag in your preheated container and set your Anova timer for 6 hours.

4. When the drumsticks are cooked, heat the butter on medium high heat.

5. Sear the drumsticks until they're brown all over.

Nutritional Info: Calories: 453, Sodium: 856 mg, Dietary Fiber: 0.3 g, Fat: 31.1 g, Carbs: 1.5 g, Protein: 40.3 g.

Filipino Adobo Chicken

This traditional Filipino dish is full of flavor thanks to sage and rosemary, and a hint of soy sauce, bay leaf, and garlic.

Servings: 2 | Prep Time: 15 Minutes | Cook Time: 4 Hours

Ingredients

1 1/2 lbs. chicken thighs and drumstick

6 pieces dried bay leaves

1 cup soy sauce

1 head garlic crushed

1 tbsp. whole peppercorn

1/4 cup vinegar

1/2 cup chicken broth

Directions

1. Preheat your Anova Precision Cooker to 155F or 68C.
2. Place the chicken and all of the other ingredients in the sous vide bag.
3. Place the bag in your preheated container and set your Anova timer for 4 hours.
4. Serve with the sauce from the bag.

Nutritional Info: Calories: 376, Sodium: 382 mg, Dietary Fiber: 1.4 g, Fat: 21.5 g, Carbs: 9.8 g, Protein 36.8 g

Curried Chicken Thighs

This recipe is filled with delicious Middle Eastern spices, but it's the curry that shines the brightest. It goes well with a side of rice.

Servings: 4 | Prep Time: 15 Minutes | Cook Time: 2 Hours

Ingredients

8 pieces boneless, skinless chicken thighs

8 garlic cloves

6 tbsp. olive oil

2 tbsp. cumin

2 tbsp. coriander

2 tsp. kosher salt

2 tsp. allspice

2 tsp. turmeric

1 tsp. ground ginger

1 tsp. ground pepper

1/4 tsp. cayenne

Directions

1. Preheat your Anova Precision Cooker to 165F or 74C.

2. Place all the ingredients except for the chicken thighs in a blender or food processor. Blend until the ingredients form a thick paste. Coat the chicken with the paste and put the chicken in the sous vide for 2 hours. Towards the end of the cooking process, preheat your broiler.

3. When the chicken is cooked, take it out of the bag and place it under the broiler. Broil each side until it browns, no more than 2 minutes per side.

Nutritional Info: Calories: 510, Sodium: 132 mg, Dietary Fiber: 1.1 g, Fat: 42 g, Carbs: 5.5 g, Protein: 39.2 g.

Maple Rosemary Turkey Breast

The dish has all the flavor of the winter months. The Rosemary gives it warmth, while the maple syrup adds a lovely sweetness.

Servings: 2 | Prep Time: 10 Minutes | Cook Time: 2 Hours

Ingredients

1 boneless turkey breast

1 tsp. salt

1/2 tsp. black pepper

1 tablespoon butter

1 tablespoon maple syrup

1/4 C shallot

2 cloves garlic

1 sprig fresh rosemary

Directions

1. Preheat your Anova Precision Cooker to 165F or 74C. Mince the garlic and julienne the shallot.

2. Season the turkey with the salt and pepper. Place the turkey and all of the other remaining ingredients in the sous vide bag.

3. Place the bag in your preheated container and set your Anova timer for 2 hours.

4. When the turkey is cooked, cut it into pieces and top with the juice from the bag.

5. Serve immediately.

Nutritional Info: Calories: 125, Sodium: 142 mg, Dietary Fiber: 1 g, Fat: 6.5 g, Carbs: 13.4 g, Protein: 4.6 g.

Chicken Tikka Masala

This is a popular dish in Indian cuisine. It's a mild curry that has just a hint of sweetness. Sous viding the sauce in a separate bag makes all the flavors come together nicely.

Servings: 2 | Prep Time: 15 Minutes | Cook Time: 2 Hours

Ingredients

4 chicken boneless skinless chicken breasts

2 tbsp. butter

pinch of salt and pepper

2 cups crushed or strained tomatoes

2 cups 18% cream

1-inch piece peeled ginger cut into chunks

4 garlic cloves

1 1/2tbsp. honey

1 tablespoon paprika

1 tablespoon cumin

3 tsp. turmeric

2 tsp. coriander

1 1/2 tsp. salt

Directions

1. Preheat your Anova Precision Cooker to 146F or 63C. Cut the ginger into chunks.

2. Salt and pepper the chicken to taste and place it in the sous vide bag with the butter. Blend all the remaining ingredients in a blender until smooth. Place the sauce in the sous vide bag.

3. Place both bags in your preheated container and set your Anova timer for 2 hours.

4. When the chicken is cooked, slice it. Then, top the chicken with the sauce and serve.

Nutritional Info: Calories: 370, Sodium: 129 mg, Dietary Fiber: 3.3 g, Fat: 12.3 g, Carbs: 36.8 g, Protein 30.5 g

8

Pork Recipes

Pulled Pork

The pulled pork has a lovely sweet and smoky flavor. You can use pulled pork in tacos, sandwiches, or on its own.

Servings: 4 | Prep Time: 10 Minutes | Cook Time: 24 Hours

Ingredients

2 lbs. boneless pork butt

1 tbsp. brown sugar

1 tbsp. fennel

1 tsp. garlic powder

2 tsp. kosher salt

1 tsp. Meyer lemon peel

1 tsp. liquid smoke

2 slices bacon

apple slices, optional

1 tsp. ground cloves, optional

Directions

1. Preheat your Anova Precision Cooker to 175F or 79C.

2. Place the pork in the sous vide bag along with all the other ingredients.

3. Place the bag in your preheated container and set your Anova timer for 12 hours.

4. When the pork is cooked, use 2 forks to shred it up.

5. Serve immediately anyway you'd like.

Nutritional Info: Calories: 459, Sodium: 132 mg, Dietary Fiber: 0.4 g, Fat: 16 g, Carbs: 3.4 g, Protein 71.1 g

Herb Rubbed Pork Chop

These pork chops are packed with flavor thanks to the herb rub and just a hint of citrus.

Servings: 4 | Prep Time: 15 Minutes | Cook Time: 2 Hours

Ingredients

4 large bone-in pork chops, about 1 1/2-inch-thick

1/4 cup parsley

10 large basil leaves

1/4 cup rosemary

1/4 cup chives

6 sprigs thyme

2 cloves garlic

zest of 1 lemon

1 tablespoon white balsamic vinegar

1/2 tsp. salt

1 tsp. fresh cracked pepper

1/4 cup extra virgin olive oil

Directions

1. Preheat your Anova Precision Cooker to 140F or 60C. Remove the stems from the rosemary and thyme. Mince the garlic.

2. Place the herbs in a food processor and pulse until finely chopped.

3. Combine the herbs with the olive oil, garlic, vinegar, salt and pepper, and lemon zest in the food processor. Blend all the ingredients until they form a smooth paste.

4. Rub the mixture all over the pork chops and place them in the sous vide bag.

5. Place the bag or bags in your preheated container and set your Anova timer for 2 hours.

6. Preheat your broiler to 550F. When the pork chops are cooked, sear the pork chops under the broiler for 3-4 minutes a side.

7. Serve the seared pork chops immediately.

Nutritional Info: Calories: 369, Sodium: 449 mg, Dietary Fiber: 4.8 g, Fat: 26.8 g, Carbs: 9.7 g, Protein 26.5 g

Honey Herbed Pork Roast

This roast takes a long time but it's worth the wait. It has a balanced aromatic flavor from the herbs and a love sweet flavor from the honey.

Servings: 3 | Prep Time: 6 hours 25 Minutes | Cook Time: 3 Hours 10 Minutes

Ingredients

8 cups water

1/3 cup honey

5 oz. kosher salt

12 bay leaves

6 sprigs rosemary

1 bunch thyme

1/2 cup garlic cloves crushed, skin left on

2 tbsp. black peppercorns

3 tbsp. olive oil

2 tbsp. vegetable oil

Directions

1. Crush the garlic and add it to the water, honey, half of both thyme and rosemary, salt, bay leaves, and peppercorns in a saucepan. Bring the mixture to a boil for 1 minute. Allow the mixture to cool.

2. Submerge the pork into the mixture in an airtight container and refrigerate for 4-6 hours.

3. Preheat your Anova Precision Cooker to 135F or 57C. Remove the stems from the thyme and rosemary leaves.

4. Place the pork in the sous vide bag with the thyme and rosemary leaves and olive oil. Make sure the pork is coated with the olive oil.

5. Place the bag in your preheated container and set your Anova timer for 3 hours.

6. When the pork is cooked, use a paper towel to pat it dry and wipe off most of the herbs.

7. Pour the vegetable oil in a skillet and heat it on high heat until it shimmers. Put in the pork and sear all sides until brown all over, a couple minutes a side.

8.   Allow the roast to rest for 10 minutes before cutting it into pieces and serving.

Nutritional Info: Calories: 376, Sodium: 183 mg, Dietary Fiber: 3.5 g, Fat: 23.9 g, Carbs: 44.9 g, Protein 2.4 g

---

Korean Style Pork Ribs

These ribs have a lovely mix of sweet and savory thanks to the brown sugar, soy, and garlic. The Sriracha adds a little heat.

Servings: 3 | Prep Time: 3 hours 15 Minutes | Cook Time: 18 Hours

Ingredients

1 rack of ribs

1/2 cup soy sauce

1/3 cup hoisin sauce

1/4 cup brown sugar

2 tbsp. sesame oil

4 garlic cloves

1/2-inch piece fresh ginger

1 to 2 tbsp. Sriracha sauce

3 tbsp. toasted sesame seeds.

6 green onions

Directions

1. Remove the membrane on the back of the ribs. Slice the ribs into 3 equal portions. Peel and grate the ginger, and peel and mince the garlic.

2. Mix everything but the ribs, green onions, and sesame seeds in a bowl using a whisk. Place the ribs in a large container or resealable plastic bag and pour in the marinade.

3. Toss the ribs in the marinade to coat and place them in the refrigerator for 3 hours. Flip the ribs halfway through refrigeration to ensure even marinating.

4. Preheat your Anova Precision Cooker to 160F or 71C. Place the ribs in the sous vide bag. Keep the left-over marinade refrigerated for later use.

5. Place the ribs in your preheated container and set your timer for 18 hours.

6. Add the reserved marinade to a saucepan and heat over medium-low heat. Allow to reduce by half.

7. Preheat your oven to 425F. When the ribs are cooked, use a brush to coat them with the glaze. Place them in the oven for 5 minutes. After 5 minutes brush them again and allow them to cook for 5 more minutes.

8. Serve immediately with a garnish of the sesame seeds and thinly sliced green onions.

Nutritional Info: Calories: 619, Sodium: 939 mg, Dietary Fiber: 1.2 g, Fat: 45.5 g, Carbs: 15.6 g, Protein 38.6 g

---

Pork Wellington

This is an incredibly simple recipe which results in an impressive dish. The sous vide and oven do the majority of the work, and you get to enjoy the flaky savory taste of the Wellington.

Servings: 2 | Prep Time: 20 Minutes | Cook Time: 5 Hours 40 Minutes

Ingredients

16-ounce pork loin

1 jar coarse ground Dijon mustard

puff pastry sheet

1 jar olive tapenade

1 tablespoon olive oil

Directions

1. Preheat your Anova Precision Cooker to 145F or 63C.

2. Coat the pork with a thin layer of the Dijon mustard. Place the pork in the sous vide bag.

3. Place the bag in your preheated container and set your Anova timer for 5 hours.

4. When the pork is almost cooked preheat your oven to 400F.

5. When the pork is cooked, pat it dry and wipe off any excess mustard. Heat oil in frying pan on high heat until shimmering and add in the pork. Sear on all sides until brown.

6. Put the pork on the pastry sheet and cover it with the tapenade. Wrap the pastry sheet around the pork. Use a fork and some warm water to seal the pastry.

7. Put the pork in the oven for 20-40 minutes. The Wellington is ready when the pastry turns golden brown.

8. Slice and serve the Wellington.

Nutritional Info: Calories: 780, Sodium: 404 mg, Dietary Fiber: 0.6 g, Fat: 51.5 g, Carbs: 11.6 g, Protein 63.7 g

BBQ Pork Ribs

These ribs will fall off the bone when they're done cooking. Use your favorite BBQ sauce for the perfect flavor.

Servings: 7 | Prep Time: 15 Minutes | Cook Time: 24 Hours 10 Minutes

Ingredients

2 tbsp. kosher salt

2 tbsp. smoked paprika

2 tbsp. light brown sugar

1 tablespoon ground cumin

1 tablespoon ground cayenne

1 tablespoon ground coriander

2 (2 1/2-lb.) racks baby back ribs

1 cup barbecue sauce

Directions

1. Preheat your Anova Precision Cooker to 155F or 68C. Cut the ribs in half crosswise.

2. Mix the spices together in a bowl. Rub the mixture on the racks of ribs.

3. Place the ribs in the bag of your choice and set your Anova timer for 24 hours.

4. Heat a grill on high heat and place the cooked ribs on the grill and cook them for 6-8 minutes until there's a good char on the ribs. Flip the ribs throughout and baste them continuously with the BBQ sauce.

5. Carve the ribs and serve immediately.

Nutritional Info: Calories: 434, Sodium: 251 mg, Dietary Fiber: 1 g, Fat: 20.4 g, Carbs: 17 g, Protein 43.1 g

Chipotle Apple Pork Loin

This makes the perfect dish to get you through the cold winter nights. The chipotle adds a little heat while the nutmeg and clove provide warmth, and the maple syrup and apple add sweetness.

Servings: 4 | Prep Time: 15 Minutes | Cook Time: 4 Hours

Ingredients

2 lbs. pork loin

1 tsp. salt

1 tsp. black pepper

1/2 tsp. chipotle powder

1/4 tsp. ground cloves

1/4 tsp. ground nutmeg

2 tbsp. apple concentrate

1 tablespoon maple syrup

1 tablespoon coconut oil

Directions

1. Preheat your Anova Precision Cooker to 134F or 57C.
2. Mix the spices together in a small bowl. Rub the mixture all over the pork. Place the pork in the sous vide bag along with maple syrup, coconut oil, and apple.
3. Place the bag in your preheated container and set your Anova timer for 4 hours.
4. When the pork is cooked, allow it to rest for a few minutes.
5. Slice the pork and serve it.

Nutritional Info: Calories: 600, Sodium: 723 mg, Dietary Fiber: 0.5 g, Fat: 35.1 g, Carbs: 5.7 g, Protein 62.1 g

Anise Seed Pork Shoulder

Pork shoulder is a cheap cut that turns very tender in the sous vide. The powerful flavor of the anise is balanced out by the sweetness of the brown sugar, and citrus from the lemon zest.

Servings: 4 | Prep Time: 10 Minutes | Cook Time: 24 Hours

Ingredients

2 lbs. boneless pork shoulder

1 medium onion,

6 medium cloves garlic

1 stick cinnamon

2 bay leaves

1 medium orange with peel

kosher salt

1 tablespoon olive oil

Directions

1. Preheat your Anova Precision Cooker to 160F or 71C.

2. Put all the ingredients in the sous vide bag and put it in your preheated container. Set your timer for 24 hours.

3. Once cooked, heat the oil in a skillet on high heat and place it in the skillet and sear it until all sides are brown. No more than 2 minutes a side.

4. Serve with the side dish of your choice.

Nutritional Info: Calories: 684, Sodium: 154 mg, Dietary Fiber: 1.3 g, Fat: 49.7 g, Carbs: 8.7 g, Protein 39.3 g

Pork Carnitas

Carnitas is a Mexican version of pulled pork that is used in tacos and various other dishes. It's alive with flavor thanks to the cinnamon, orange, bay leaf, and garlic.

Servings: 8 | Prep Time: 30 Minutes | Cook Time: 12 Hours

Ingredients

4 lbs. boneless pork shoulder

1 medium onion,

6 medium cloves garlic

1 stick cinnamon

2 bay leaves

1 medium orange with peel

kosher salt

Directions

1. Preheat your Anova Precision Cooker to 165F or 74C. Cut the pork into 2-inch-thick slabs. Roughly chop the onion and break the cinnamon into 3 pieces. Slice the orange into quarters.

2. Mix the garlic, onion, cinnamon, bay leaf, and pork in a large bowl. Juice the orange in the bowl and add the orange pieces. Salt the pork to taste.

3. Put everything in the sous vide bag and place in the preheated container. Set your Anova timer for 12 hours.

4. When the pork is cooked, open the bag and empty it in a bowl. Preheat your broiler to high. Use tongs to take the pork out of the bowl and place it on a rimmed baking sheet. Use 2 forks to shred the pork.

5. Broil the pork for about 10 minutes. Flip the pork throughout the process. The pork is ready when it's brown and crispy.

6. Serve with tortillas and your favorite condiments.

Nutritional Info: Calories: 682, Sodium: 156 mg, Dietary Fiber: 1.1 g, Fat: 48.6 g, Carbs: 4.7 g, Protein 53.5 g

Soy Ginger Pork Belly

Pork belly is a fatty and inexpensive cut of pork that's full of flavor. This recipe uses Asian flavors to enhance the rich fatty belly.

Servings: 3 | Prep Time: 15 Minutes | Cook Time: 48 Hours

Ingredients

1 1/2 lbs. fresh pork belly

3 star-anise

6 slices of ginger

1/4 cup Chinese soy sauce

1 1/2 cups of dark brown sugar

Directions

1. Preheat your Anova Precision Cooker to 140F or 60C.
2. Cut the belly into 3 equal parts. Mix the soy sauce and brown sugar in a bowl.
3. Place the pork belly in the sous vide bag with the soy sauce mixture and cook for 48 hours.
4. When the pork is cooked, pour the liquid in the bag through a sieve into a pot.
5. Heat the sauce on high heat until it thickens into a glaze.
6. Heat a skillet on high heat and sear the pork until it browns.
7. Place a smear of the glaze on your serving plate and then top the pork with the glaze.

Nutritional Info: Calories: 409, Sodium: 38 mg, Dietary Fiber: 0.3 g, Fat: 24.3 g, Carbs: 44.1 g, Protein 4.6 g

Maple Pepper Pork Chop

The brine ensures that you get the juiciest and tender pork chop possible. The maple and pepper give it a nice balance of sweet and spicy.

Servings: 4 | Prep Time: 4 Minutes | Cook Time: 1 Hour

Ingredients

4 pork chops

2 cups hot water

1/2 cup + 2 tbsp. salt

1/4 cup honey

8 bay leaves

1/2 bunch thyme

1/2 cup garlic cloves

2 tbsp. peppercorns

6 tbsp. vegetable oil

1/2 cup granulated maple sugar,

2 tbsp. kosher salt

1 tablespoon granulated garlic

2 tsp. ground black pepper

1 tsp. red pepper flakes

Directions

1. Crush the garlic and leave the skin on. Pour the water in a large pot. Add in the salt, and honey. Stir the mixture until everything dissolves.

2. Add 6 cups of room temperature water. Pour in the garlic, thyme, peppercorns and bay leaf. Put the pork chop in the pot and refrigerator for 4 hours, stir the pot half way through.

3. In the last few minutes of the brining process, heat a skillet on high heat. Pour 2 tbsp. of oil in the skillet.

4. Sear the pork chops for 1 minute per side. Allow the pork chops to cool for a bit.

5. Mix together the remaining ingredients. Preheat your Anova Precision Cooker to 144F or 62C.

6. Season the pork chop with about 1 tsp. of the mixture per side. Place the pork chops in the bag of your choice along with 2 tbsp. of oil.

7. Place the bag in your preheated container and set your Anova timer for 45 minutes.

8. Heat 2 tbsp. of oil in a skillet on high heat. Sear the pork chops for 45 second per side, seasoning the chops with some of the leftover mixture.

9. Serve immediately.

Nutritional Info: Calories: 563, Sodium: 355 mg, Dietary Fiber: 2.7 g, Fat: 40.9 g, Carbs: 32 g, Protein 20.9 g

---

"Smokeless" Smoked Ribs

The ribs aren't smoked but they taste like they are because of the mustard and liquid smoke. The rub perfectly complements the smoked flavor of the ribs.

Servings: 3 | Prep Time: 15 Minutes | Cook Time: 10 Hours

Ingredients

1 rack of baby back ribs

1/4 cup yellow mustard

1/4 cup liquid smoke

1 cup BBQ sauce

1 oz. brown sugar

3 oz. salt

1 oz. chili powder

1 oz. garlic powder

1 oz. onion powder

.75 ground black pepper

1/2 oz. smoke paprika

1 oz. cayenne powder

Directions

1. Preheat your Anova Precision Cooker to 165F or 74C.
2. Cut the ribs into 3 equal portions. Mix together all the spices. Mix together the liquid smoke and yellow mustard in a small bowl.
3. Coat the ribs with mustard mixture and then 1/2 cup of the dry mixture.
4. Place the ribs in the sous vide bag and put the bag in your preheated container. Set your Anova timer for 9 hours.
5. Preheat your grill so half the grill is on high heat and the other half is medium-low.
6. When the ribs are cooked, place them on the cooler side of the grill with the meat side up. Coat the meat side with the BBQ sauce.
7. Close the grill and allow the ribs to cook for 5 minutes. Add another coat of BBQ sauce and allow them to cook for 5 more minutes. Remove the ribs from the grill.
8. Allow the ribs to rest for about 10 minutes before serving.

Nutritional Info: Calories: 946, Sodium: 595 mg, Dietary Fiber: 4.2 g, Fat: 74.2 g, Carbs: 18.2 g, Protein 51 g

Carolina BBQ Pulled Pork

This pulled pork has a different flavor than you're probably used to. Carolina style BBQ uses a vinegar-based sauce which gives it a tangy flavor.

Servings: 6 | Prep Time: 24 Hours 30 Minutes | Cook Time: 10 Hours

Ingredients

3 lbs. pork butt

2 tbsp. vegetable oil

1/4 cup cumin

1/4 cup brown sugar

1/2 cup paprika

1/4 cup chili powder

1 tablespoon cayenne powder

1/4 cup salt

1/4 cup fresh ground black pepper,

1 tsp. onion powder

1 tsp. garlic powder

1 cup white vinegar

1 cup apple cider vinegar

1/2 cup packed brown sugar,

1 tsp. cayenne pepper

1 tablespoon red pepper flakes

1 tsp. salt

1 tsp. fresh ground pepper

Directions

1. Mix the last 7 ingredients in a pot and heat it on medium heat until the sugar dissolves. Place the mixture in the refrigerator covered for 24 hours.

2. Combine the remaining spices in a bowl. Rub the mixture all over the pork. Place the pork on a large container and refrigerate at least overnight and up to 24 hours.

3. Preheat your Anova Precision Cooker to 165F or 74C. Place the pork in the sous vide bag.

4. Place the bag in your preheated cooker and set your timer for 18 hours.

5. Place the oil in a skillet and heat on high heat until it shimmers. Add the pork and sear on all sides until it browns. This should take 1-2 minutes per side.

6. Use 2 forks to shred the pork. Warm the sauce over medium low heat on the stove.

7. Top the pork with the sauce and serve.

Nutritional Info: Calories: 652, Sodium: 203 mg, Dietary Fiber: 8.3 g, Fat: 23.3 g, Carbs: 35.2 g, Protein 74.6 g

---

Bourbon Glazed Pork Tenderloin

This recipe has a delicious complex flavor. The spices add savory flavors, while the glaze imparts a sweet caramel flavor for balance.

Servings: 4 | Prep Time: 40 Minutes | Cook Time: 3 Hours 15 minutes

Ingredients

2 lbs. pork tenderloin

1 tsp. dried sage

1 tsp. allspice

1/2 tsp. ginger

fresh ground pepper

1 cup bourbon whiskey

1/2 cup brown sugar

1/2 cup ketchup

2 tsp. Worcester sauce

1 tsp. liquid smoke

1/4 cup apple juice

Directions

1. Preheat your Anova Precision Cooker to 135F or 57C. Combine the sage, ginger, allspice, and pepper to taste.

2. Rub the mixture on the pork and place it in the sous vide bag.

3. Place the bag in your preheated container and set timer for 3 hours.

4. Put all the remaining ingredients in pot and allow them to come to a simmer on medium high heat. Cook the sauce for around 30 minutes, until it thickens. Stir occasionally throughout the cooking process.

5. When the pork is cooked, take it out of the bag and preheat a grill to high heat. Place the pork on the grill.

6. Coat the top side with glaze and sear the bottom until grill marks are present. Flip and repeat the process. Keep flipping and coating the pork a few more times.

7. Searing each side for no more than 60 seconds. Take pork off the grill.

8. Glaze the pork again before cutting it and serve.

Nutritional Info: Calories: 453, Sodium: 470 mg, Dietary Fiber: 0.3 g, Fat: 8.2 g, Carbs: 28.5 g, Protein 60 g

Sweet and Sour Pork Belly

This has an authentic flavor you would expect to find at a Chinese restaurant. The pork belly is so tender and goes well with rice.

Servings: 4 | Prep Time: 10 Minutes | Cook Time: 48 Hours

Ingredients

2 lbs. skinless, boneless pork belly

6 scallions

1/4 cup honey

1/4 cup soy sauce

3 tbsp. sambal oelek

1 tablespoon grape seed or other neutral oil

Directions

1. Preheat your Anova Precision Cooker to 140F or 60C. Slice the scallions into 1-inch pieces and the pork belly crosswise into 2-inch-wide pieces.

2. Place all the ingredients except the oil in the sous vide bag and turn the bag to coat the pork.

3. Place the bag in your preheated container and set your Anova timer for 10 hours.

4. When the pork is cooked, place the oil in a skillet and heat it on medium high heat until it's very hot. Use a paper towel to pat the pork dry before placing it in the skillet. Sear the pork on all sides for about 30 seconds a side.

5. Serve immediately.

Nutritional Info: Calories: 672, Sodium: 101 mg, Dietary Fiber: 0.8 g, Fat: 60.5 g, Carbs: 20.7 g, Protein 12.1 g

Southwestern Rubbed Pork Tenderloin

This pork tenderloin has deep, robust flavors. The chili powder is bold, and the chipotle gives a nice amount of heat to the dish.

Servings: 3 | Prep Time: 15 Minutes | Cook Time: 3 Hours

Ingredients

1 lb. pork tenderloin

2 tsp. lemon juice

1 tsp. chili powder

1/2 tsp. garlic powder

1/4 tsp. chipotle

1 tsp. salt

1/2 tsp. pepper

1 tablespoon olive oil

Directions

1. Preheat your Anova Precision Cooker to 135F or 57C. Trim any excess fat off the pork.

2. Coat the pork with the lemon juice. Combine all the spices in a bowl and rub the mixture on the pork.

3. Place the pork in the sous vide bag and put it in your preheated container. Set your Anova timer for 3 hours.

4. Heat the oil in a skillet on medium high heat. Put it in the skillet and sear for about 3-4 minutes per side. Allow the pork to rest for 5-10 minutes before slicing.

5. Slice the pork and serve.

Nutritional Info: Calories: 262, Sodium: 87 mg, Dietary Fiber: 0.5 g, Fat: 10.2 g, Carbs: 1.1 g, Protein 39.8 g

9

Side Dishes

Green Beans Almandine

This is a light and easy side dish to prepare. The green beans come out crispy, and the lemon adds citrusy freshness with a crunchy element thanks to the almonds.

Servings: 3 | Prep Time: 15 Minutes | Cook Time: 1 Hour 30 Minutes

Ingredients

3 cups fresh green beans

2 tbsp. olive oil

1 tablespoon lemon zest

1 tsp. salt

2 tbsp. lemon juice

1/2 cup toasted almonds

Directions

1. Preheat your Anova Precision Cooker to 180F or 82C. Clean and trim the green beans and mix with lemon zest and olive oil. Roughly chop the almonds.

2. Place the whole mixture in the sous vide bag and place in your preheated container. Set the Anova timer for 1 1/2 hours.

3. Put the cooked green beans on a plate, top with lemon juice, and season with salt.

4. Mix in the almonds and serve.

Nutritional Info: Calories: 209, Sodium: 78 mg, Dietary Fiber: 5.9 g, Fat: 17.5 g, Carbs: 11.9 g, Protein 5.5 g

Apple Butternut Squash Soup

This sweet soup takes minimal effort, and your sous vide cooks the apples and butternut squash to a perfect consistency for silky smooth soup.

Servings: 4 | Prep Time: 10 Minutes | Cook Time: 2 Hour

Ingredients

1 medium butternut squash,

1 large tart apple

1/2 yellow onion

1 tsp. sea salt

3/4 cups light cream

Directions

1. Preheat your Anova Precision Cooker to 185F or 85C. Core and slice the apple, peel and slice the butternut squash, slice the onion.

2. Place the butternut squash, apple, and onion in a sous vide bag. Place the bag in your preheated container and set your Anova timer for 2 hours.

3. Once cooked, place the ingredients in a blender and blend until smooth. Add the remaining ingredients and puree again.

Nutritional Info: Calories: 226, Sodium: 48 mg, Dietary Fiber: 7.2 g, Fat: 7.3 g, Carbs: 42.4 g, Protein 3.6 g

Sweet Potato Casserole with a Pretzel Crust

This is a perfect side dish for the holidays. The sweet potato is balanced by the salty pretzels.

Servings: 4 | Prep Time: 10 Minutes | Cook Time: 2 Hours 20 Minutes

Ingredients

5 cups diced sweet potatoes

4 tbsp. plus 2 tbsp. unsalted butter, divided

pinch of cinnamon

1/4 tsp. ground nutmeg

1 1/2 tsp. kosher salt

pinch ground white pepper,

2 tbsp. crème fraiche

1 cup crushed pretzels

Directions

1. Preheat your Anova Precision Cooker to 180F or 82C. Crush the pretzels, and peel and dice the sweet potatoes. The potatoes should be diced into medium sized chunks. Melt the butter.

2. Put the potatoes in the sous vide bag along with the cinnamon, nutmeg, salt, white pepper, and 4 tbsp. of butter. Place the bag in your preheated container and set your timer for 2 hours.

3. When the potatoes are almost cooked, preheat your oven to 400F. Crush the pretzels if you haven't done so.

4. Rice or mash the potatoes, mix in the crème fraiche, and place the mixture in a casserole dish. Melt the remaining butter.

5. Mix the melted butter with the pretzels and top the casserole with pretzels.

6. Cook the casserole for 20 minutes or until it starts to brown and bubbles.

Nutritional Info: Calories: 354, Sodium: 76 mg, Dietary Fiber: 7.8 g, Fat: 14.5 g, Carbs: 53.8 g, Protein 3.3 g

Glazed Carrots

This is a classic dish that goes with just about anything. The carrots come out tasting so creamy and sweet you'll almost want them for dessert.

Servings: 4 | Prep Time: 10 Minutes | Cook Time: 20 Minutes

Ingredients

1 lb. baby carrots

2 tsp. butter

2 tsp. honey

salt and pepper

Directions

1. Preheat your Anova Precision Cooker to 185F or 84C.

2. Place all the ingredients in the sous vide bag including salt and pepper to taste.

3. Place the bag in your preheated container and set your Anova timer for 1 hour.

4. When the carrots are cooked, put them on a plate to cool for a few minutes.

5. Serve with your main dish.

Nutritional Info: Calories: 67, Sodium: 10 mg, Dietary Fiber: 3.3 g, Fat: 2.1 g, Carbs: 12.2 g, Protein 0.8 g

Buttery Asparagus

The flavor of the asparagus is front and center here. The asparagus comes out nice and crispy and the garlic powder enhances its natural flavor.

Servings: 2 | Prep Time: 10 Minutes | Cook Time: 15 Minutes

Ingredients

12 oz. asparagus

2 - 3 tbsp. butter

1 tsp. garlic powder

salt and pepper

Directions

1. Preheat your Anova Precision Cooker to 185F or 85C.

2. Place the ingredients in the sous vide bag and put it in your preheated container. Set your timer for 15 minutes.

3. Take the cooked asparagus out of the bag and serve immediately.

Nutritional Info: Calories: 160, Sodium: 4 mg, Dietary Fiber: 3.8 g, Fat: 14.2 g, Carbs: 7.8 g, Protein 4.1 g

Maple Orange Beets

Beets have a wonderful earthy flavor with just the right amount of sweetness. This recipe combines the complex flavor of beets with the vibrant citrus notes of fresh orange.

Servings: 4 | Prep Time: 15 Minutes | Cook Time: 1 Hours 10 Minutes

Ingredients

1 large beet

1 orange slice

1/2 tsp. maple syrup

salt and pepper

goat cheese for garnish

Directions

1. Preheat your Anova Precision Cooker to 183F or 84C. Cut the top and bottom off the beet and peel it. Slice the beet into medium size chunks.

2. Place the beets in the sous vide bag with the other ingredients, and salt and pepper to taste.

3. Place the beets in your preheated container and set your Anova timer for 1 hour.

4. When the beets are cooked, heat a skillet on medium heat and pour in the beets and any liquid in the bag. Allow them to cook until the liquids thicken into a glaze.

5. Pour everything onto a plate and top with goat cheese to serve.

Nutritional Info: Calories: 18, Sodium: 19 mg, Dietary Fiber: 1.3 g, Fat: 0.1 g, Carbs: 6.9 g, Protein 0.7 g

Bacon Gruyere Quiche Cups

These individual quiches are perfect for entertaining or a fun snack any time. All you need is 6 mini mason jars and you're ready to go.

Servings: 6 | Prep Time: 30 Minutes | Cook Time: 1 Hour 30 Minutes

Ingredients

6 oz. bacon

3 tbsp. butter

2 large shallots

1 bay leaf

10 eggs

1 1/3 cups half and half

1 cup gruyere cheese

2 tsp. salt

1/2 tsp. pepper freshly ground

1/2 tsp. nutmeg ground

1/4 tsp. cayenne pepper ground

Directions

1. Shred the gruyere, thinly slice the shallots, and slice the bacon into 1/2-inch pieces.

2. Put the butter, bacon, shallots, thyme, and bay leaf in a skillet and heat on medium heat.

3. Cook until the butter melts, around 5 minutes, stir occasionally. Lower the heat to low and cook for around 20 more minutes, until the bacon is fully cooked. Stir occasionally throughout the 20 minutes. Allow the mixture to cool for 30 minutes.

4. Preheat your Anova Precision Cooker to 170F or 76C. Use a blender to puree the eggs on medium speed, until the eggs foam. Add the cayenne, nutmeg, half and half, and pepper. Blend again until smooth.

5. Divide the bacon mixture between 6 mini mason jars. Add the eggs and top with cheese. Run the jars under hot water.

6. Place the jars in your preheated container and set your Anova timer for 1 hour and 30 minutes.

7. Place a towel on the counter before taking the jars out of the container.

8.   Place the cooked jars on the towel and allow them to cool for a few minutes before serving.

Nutritional Info: Calories: 458, Sodium: 165 mg, Dietary Fiber: 0.1 g, Fat: 37 g, Carbs: 4.2 g, Protein 26.9 g

---

Garlic and Rosemary Risotto

This makes a creamy and delicious risotto without all the stirring. It has a lovely aromatic flavor thanks to the garlic and rosemary.

Servings: 4 | Prep Time: 10 Minutes | Cook Time: 45 Minutes

Ingredients

1 cup Arborio rice

1 tsp. extra virgin olive oil

2 tbsp. jarred roasted minced garlic

3 cups chicken or vegetable broth

1 sprig fresh rosemary

salt and pepper

1/3 cup grated Romano cheese

Directions

1. Preheat your Anova Precision Cooker to 185F or 85C. Discard the stems from the rosemary and mince the leaves.

2. Place all ingredients except for cheese in a resealable bag.

3. Place the bag in your preheated container and set your Anova timer for 45 minutes.

4. When the rice is cooked, place it in a bowl and fluff with a fork.

5. Mix in the cheese and serve immediately.

Nutritional Info: Calories: 228, Sodium: 105 mg, Dietary Fiber: 1.7 g, Fat: 3.2 g, Carbs: 40.5 g, Protein 7.9 g

Feta and Roasted Red Pepper Egg Bites

These are just like the egg bites at Starbucks but made for a fraction of the price. You need 6 mini mason jars to make this dish.

Servings: 6 | Prep Time: 10 Minutes | Cook Time: 1 Hour

Ingredients

6 large eggs

1 tablespoon sour cream

1/2 cup crumbled feta cheese

1/2 tsp. kosher salt

1/8 tsp. ground black pepper

1/8 tsp. dried crushed red pepper

1/4 cup roasted red peppers

2 tbsp. fresh basil

Directions

1. Preheat your Anova Precision Cooker to 172F or 78C. Finely chop the basil and roasted red peppers.

2. Place the eggs, crushed red pepper, salt, sour cream, feta, and pepper in a food processor or blender. Puree the ingredients on medium speed until smooth. Add the red peppers and basil then pulse quickly to mix everything.

3. Lightly coat the inside of the jars with cooking spray. Put an equal amount of the egg mixture in each jar.

4. Place the jars in your preheated container and set your Anova timer for 1 hour.

5. When the eggs are cooked, slide a butter knife around the inside of the jar to loosen the egg bites. Set the jars upside down so the egg bites can slide out of the jar.

Nutritional Info: Calories: 111, Sodium: 423 mg, Dietary Fiber: 0.1 g, Fat: 8.1 g, Carbs: 1.5 g, Protein 1.2 g

Turkey and Mushroom Risotto

This is a great way to use leftover turkey or chicken if turkey isn't available. The mushrooms give it a nice earthly flavor.

Servings: 4 | Prep Time: 15 Minutes | Cook Time: 45 Minutes

Ingredients

1 cup Arborio rice

1 tsp. extra virgin olive oil

1 small yellow onion

8 - 10 Crimini mushrooms

8 oz. cooked turkey or chicken

2 tbsp. jarred roasted minced garlic

720 ml turkey or chicken broth

1 sprig fresh rosemary,

salt and pepper to taste

1/3 cup grated Romano cheese

Directions

1. Preheat your Anova Precision Cooker to 183F or 83C. Clean and slice the mushrooms, and peel and dice the onion. Dice the turkey or chicken.

2. Heat the olive oil in a pan over medium heat. Add the mushrooms, and onions. Sauté the ingredients until they're tender, about 6 minutes.

3. Place all the ingredients except for the cheese in a sous vide bag.

4. Place the bag in your preheated container and set your Anova timer for 45 minutes.

5. When the rice is cooked, place it in a bowl, and fluff with a fork.

6. Mix in the cheese and serve immediately.

Nutritional Info: Calories: 308, Sodium: 829 mg, Dietary Fiber: 2 g, Fat: 4.9 g, Carbs: 41.4 g, Protein 23.1 g

Artichoke Heart and Roasted Red Pepper Risotto

This recipe combines both subtle and intense flavors. The artichokes add a mild earthiness while the roasted peppers add an intense, rich, smoky flavor.

Servings: 4 | Prep Time: 10 Minutes | Cook Time: 1 Hour

Ingredients

1 cup Arborio rice

3 cups vegetable or chicken broth

1 can artichoke hearts, chopped

1 (12-oz) jar roasted red peppers, chopped

1 tablespoon extra-virgin olive oil

4 cloves garlic minced

1 tsp. Italian seasoning

ground black pepper

1/2 cup grated parmesan cheese

Directions

1. Preheat your Anova Precision Cooker to 183F or 83C.

2. Place all the ingredients except for the cheese in a sous vide bag.

3. Place the bag in your preheated container and set your Anova timer for 1 hour.

4. When the rice is cooked, place it in a bowl or on a plate, and fluff with a fork.

5. Mix in the cheese and serve immediately.

Nutritional Info: Calories: 259, Sodium: 631 mg, Dietary Fiber: 3.6 g, Fat: 5.2 g, Carbs: 44.3 g, Protein 8.4 g

Toasted Quinoa with Garlic

Quinoa is a protein packed grain that comes out perfectly fluffy from the sous vide. The garlic adds a lovely depth of flavor.

Servings: 4 | Prep Time: 15 Minutes | Cook Time: 1 Hour

Ingredients

1 cup white quinoa

2 cloves garlic minced

1 bay leaf

kosher salt

1 1/2 cups water

Directions

1. Preheat your Anova Precision Cooker to 180F or 82C. Rinse the quinoa thoroughly.

2. Place the quinoa in a pan and heat on medium heat. Stir constantly until the quinoa browns

3. Place all the ingredients in a sous vide bag.

4. Place the bag in your preheated container and set your timer for 1 hour.

5. When the quinoa is cooked, place it in a bowl and fluff with a fork. Discard the garlic and bay leaf. Add salt to taste.

Nutritional Info: Calories: 160, Sodium: 4 mg, Dietary Fiber: 3.1 g, Fat: 2.6 g, Carbs: 28.1 g, Protein 6.1 g

Perfect Farro

Farro is an ancient Italian grain that's been getting a lot of buzz. It has a lovely nutty flavor that pairs well with nearly anything.

Servings: 2 | Prep Time: 15 Minutes | Cook Time: 1 Hour

Ingredients

---

6 oz. farro, rinsed

12 oz. water or broth

2 big pinches of salt

Directions

---

1. Preheat your Anova Precision Cooker to 190F or 88C. Soak the farro stirring occasionally.

2. Place all the ingredients in a sous vide bag.

3. Place the bag in your preheated container and set your Anova timer for 1 hour.

4. When the farro is cooked, drain any excess liquid. Fluff the farro with a fork and serve immediately.

Nutritional Info: Calories: 300, Sodium: 5 mg, Dietary Fiber: 10.5 g, Fat: 2.3 g, Carbs: 55.5 g, Protein 10.5 g

---

Lemon and Parmesan Broccoli

The broccoli comes out crispy and yet tender. The lemon adds a bright citrus flavor that's balanced by the saltiness of the parmesan.

Servings: 5 | Prep Time: 10 Minutes | Cook Time: 45 Minutes

Ingredients

1 head of broccoli

2 tbsp. butter

salt and pepper

parmesan cheese for sprinkling

1 lemon

Directions

1. Preheat your Anova Precision Cooker to 185F or 85C. Cut the head of broccoli into large pieces.

2. Put the broccoli and butter in a sous vide bag. Salt and pepper to taste.

3. Place the bag in your preheated container and set your Anova timer for 45 minutes.

4. Transfer broccoli to a plate and add the lemon juice and top with cheese to serve.

Nutritional Info: Calories: 63, Sodium: 51 mg, Dietary Fiber: 4.7 g, Fat: 4.8 g, Carbs: 4.7 g, Protein 1.7 g

Soft Poached Eggs

Poaching eggs can be a hassle, because it's so easy to over or undercook them. These come out great every time with a slightly runny yolk.

Servings: 4 | Prep Time: 5 Minutes | Cook Time: 15 Minutes

Ingredients

4 large eggs

Salt and pepper

Directions

1. Preheat your Anova Precision Cooker to 167F or 75C.

2. Use a slotted spoon to carefully put the eggs in your preheated container. Set your Anova timer for 15 minutes

3. While the eggs are cooking, prepare an ice bath

4. Let the eggs cool in the ice bath for around a minute. Crack the eggs in a bowl or on your preferred surface like a piece of toast.

5. Salt and pepper to taste and serve.

Nutritional Info: Calories: 63, Sodium: 10 mg, Dietary Fiber: 0 g, Fat: 4.4 g,
Carbs: 0.3 g, Protein 5.5 g

Scrambled Eggs

These sous vide scrambled eggs always come out velvety and almost custard like. The have a rich, creamy flavor the whole family will love.

Servings: 2 | Prep Time: 10 Minutes | Cook Time: 15 Minutes

Ingredients

6 large eggs

2 tbsp. whole milk

2 tbsp. heavy cream

2 tbsp. unsalted butter plus
2 tbsp. unsalted butter
divided

salt and pepper

Directions

1. Preheat your Anova Precision Cooker to 165F or 74C. Melt 2 tbsp. of butter in a small pan and keep it warm. Soften the other 2 tbsp. of butter.

2. Whisk the eggs, cream, and milk in a bowl. Then add in the melted butter, whisking the entire time. Salt and pepper to taste.

3. Put the mixture in the sous vide bag of your choice and place it in your preheated container. Set your timer for 15 minutes.

4. Take the eggs out of the container about every 3-5 minutes to give them a quick massage. While they're cooking, heat the other 2 tbsp. of butter on medium heat. Once it melts, stir constantly until it turns brown. This should take around 5 minutes.

5. Strain the brown butter and plate the cooked eggs. Top with brown butter to serve.

Nutritional Info: Calories: 377, Sodium: 30 mg, Dietary Fiber: 0 g, Fat: 32.5 g, Carbs: 2.3 g, Protein 19.8 g

Sweet and Smoky Butternut Squash

Butternut squash has a sweet flavor that's intensified by the brown sugar and vanilla. The liquid smoke and paprika add a rich smokiness that balances the sweetness.

Servings: 4 | Prep Time: 15 Minutes | Cook Time: 1 hour

Ingredients

1/2 lb. butternut squash

3.5 oz. cooked bacon bits

1/4 cup brown sugar

1 tablespoon paprika

1 tsp. liquid smoke

1 tsp. vanilla extract

salt and black pepper

Directions

1. Preheat your Anova Precision Cooker to 185F or 85C. Remove the seeds from the squash peel it and cut it into cubes

2. Mix all the ingredients in a bowl, adding salt and pepper to taste.

3. Place the mixture in a sous vide bag.

4. Place the bag in your preheated container and set your Anova timer for 1 hour and serve immediately.

Nutritional Info: Calories: 202, Sodium: 57 mg, Dietary Fiber: 1.8 g, Fat: 10.7 g, Carbs: 17 g, Protein 10 g

10

Dessert

Buttered Spiced Apples

This is a perfect dessert for the winter months. The spices have a warm flavor that are comforting on cold winter nights.

Servings: 6 | Prep Time: 20 Minutes | Cook Time: 2 Hour

Ingredients

Zest and juice from 1 lemon

6 small apples

6 tbsp. unsalted butter

1/2 tsp. salt

1/2 tsp. ground cinnamon

1/4 tsp. ground nutmeg

1 heaping tsp. dark brown sugar

1 heaping tablespoon dark or golden raisins

Dollops of crème fraîche, whipped cream or ice cream

Directions

1. Preheat your Anova Precision Cooker to 170F or 77C. Peel and core the apples, soften the butter, and completely zest the lemon.

2. Coat the apples with lemon juice. Place the lemon zest in a bowl and combine with the cinnamon, sugar, nutmeg, raisins, butter, and salt. Place an equal amount of the mixture in the hollowed-out center of each apple.

3. Put 2 apples in each bag and set your Anova timer for 2 hours.

4. Remove apples from the bag and serve immediately with cooking liquid.

Nutritional Info: Calories: 229, Sodium: 278 mg, Dietary Fiber: 5.9 g, Fat: 12 g, Carbs: 33.9 g, Protein 0.9 g

Champagne Strawberries

These strawberries have the most intense strawberry flavor you can imagine. They're great on their own or served with ice creams, meringues, or whipped cream.

Servings: 4 | Prep Time: 10 Minutes | Cook Time: 15 Minutes

Ingredients

12 oz. strawberries trimmed   2 tsp. sugar

2 tbsp. champagne

Directions

1.   Preheat your Anova Precision Cooker to 185F or 85F.

2.   Place all the ingredients in a sous vide bag and place the bag in the preheated container and set your Anova timer for 15 minutes.

3.   Meanwhile, prepare an ice bath. When the strawberries are cooked, put them directly in the ice bath until they're cold.

Nutritional Info: Calories: 80, Sodium: 1 mg, Dietary Fiber: 1.7 g, Fat: 12 g, Carbs: 0.3 g, Protein 0.6 g

Red Wine Poached Pears

Bosc pears pick up the delicious flavor of the red wine better than other pears. This recipe allows you to have perfect, soft poached pears every time.

Servings: 4 | Prep Time: 10 Minutes | Cook Time: 1 Hour

Ingredients

4 ripe Bosc pears

1 cup red wine

1/2 cup granulated sugar

1/4 cup sweet vermouth

1 tsp. salt

3 (3-inch pieces) orange zest

1 vanilla bean

vanilla ice cream

Directions

1. Preheat your Anova Precision Cooker to 175F or 79C. Peel the pear and scrape the vanilla bean seeds.

2. Put everything except for the ice cream in a sous vide bag. Then, place the bag in the preheated container and set your Anova timer for 1 hour.

3. When the pears are cooked, slice them up and core them. Reserve the juices from the bag.

4. Place the sliced pears in 4 bowls and add a scoop of ice cream. Top with the reserved juices and serve.

Nutritional Info: Calories: 299, Sodium: 606 mg, Dietary Fiber: 7.1 g, Fat: 0.3 g, Carbs: 66.2 g, Protein 1 g

Rose Water Apricots

Apricots have an amazing, velvety texture when they're cooked sous vide. The rose water adds a floral flavor that complements the sweet apricots.

Servings: 8 | Prep Time: 10 Minutes | Cook Time: 1 Hour

Ingredients

8 apricots   1/2 cup of water

1 tsp. rosewater

Directions

1. Preheat your Anova Precision Cooker to 180F or 82F. Cut the apricots in half and remove the pit.

2. Place all the ingredients in a sous vide bag. Then, place the bag in your preheated container and set your Anova timer for 1 hour.

3. When the peaches are cooked, serve in a small bowl or plate.

Nutritional Info: Calories: 17, Sodium: 1 mg, Dietary Fiber: 0.7 g, Fat: 0.2 g, Carbs: 3.8 g, Protein 0.5 g

Dolce De Leche

This recipe couldn't be any easier, you put the condensed milk in your sous vide and let it cook for 13 hours. The result is a beautifully rich, silk caramel that you'll love.

Servings: 8 | Prep Time: 5 Minutes | Cook Time: 13 Hour

Ingredients

12 oz. sweetened condensed milk

Directions

1.   Preheat your Anova Precision Cooker to 185F or 85F.
2.   Put the milk in a sous vide bag or a pint size mason jar.
3.   Put the bag or mason jar in your preheated container and set your Anova timer for 13 hours.
4.   When the dolce de leche is cooked, pour it into 4 bowls to serve.

Nutritional Info: Calories: 91, Sodium: 36 mg, Dietary Fiber: 0 g, Fat: 2.5 g, Carbs: 15.4 g, Protein 2.2 g

Champagne Zabaglione

Zabaglione is an Italian custard dessert that's packed with flavor. This recipe is pretty boozy so it's probably not for kids.

Servings: 4 | Prep Time: 20 Minutes | Cook Time: 1 Hour

Ingredients

4 large egg yolks

1/2 cup superfine sugar

1/2 cup champagne

1/2 cup heavy whipping cream

1/2-pint fresh raspberries

Directions

1. Preheat your Anova Precision Cooker to 165F or 74F.

2. Place the eggs in a bowl and slowly whisk in the sugar. Continue to whisk until ingredients become thick. Add the champagne and continue to lightly whisk until you have dissolved the sugar.

3. Place the mixture in a sous vide bag. Then, place the bag in the preheated container. Set your Anova timer for 20 minutes.

4. Meanwhile, prepare an ice bath. Once cooked, put the bag in the ice bath until cold. Whip the cream and fold the whipped cream into the cold zabaglione.

5. Place a layer of the mixture in a glass and then top with some berries. Add another layer of the mixture and top with a couple more berries. Repeat the process with 3 more glasses.

6. Serve immediately

Nutritional Info: Calories: 231, Sodium: 14 mg, Dietary Fiber: 2.5 g, Fat: 10.3 g, Carbs: 30.8 g, Protein 3.5 g

Mexican Pot De Creme

These custard like pots have a creamy texture and a deep chocolate flavor that's enhanced by the cinnamon and balanced by a pinch of salt.

Servings: 5 | Prep Time: 2 Hours 40 Minutes | Cook Time: 30 Minutes

Ingredients

1 cup heavy whipping cream

1/2 cup whole milk

1 cup bittersweet chocolate, chopped

1/2 tsp. cinnamon

1 tablespoon sugar

3 egg yolks

2 tsp. cocoa powder

1/2 tsp. vanilla extract

1/8 tsp. salt

flakey sea salt for garnish

5 (4-oz) mason jars

Directions

1. Preheat your Anova Precision Cooker to 180F or 82C. Chop the chocolate and put it in a large bowl with the sugar and cinnamon.

2. Heat a pan on medium heat with the cream and milk. Allow the mixture to come to a boil and then pour it over the chocolate. Let the mixture rest for 5 minutes.

3. While the mixture is resting, whisk together the vanilla, salt, cocoa powder, and eggs.

4. Stir the chocolate mixture. Whisk in the cocoa powder mixture into the chocolate mixture.

5. Pour an equal amount of the mixture into the mason jars. Place the mason jars in your preheated container and set your Anova timer for 30 minutes.

6. When the jars are cooked, place them on top of a kitchen towel on the counter to cool for 20 minutes. Place the cooled jars in the refrigerator for at least 2 hours.

7. Sprinkle the jars with a little sea salt to serve.

Nutritional Info: Calories: 332, Sodium: 109 mg, Dietary Fiber: 1.5 g, Fat: 22.4 g, Carbs: 25.1 g, Protein 5.6 g

----

Lavender Spiced Crème Brulèè

Cooking your crème brûlée in a sous vide gives it the perfect texture every time. The lavender adds a light floral flavor.

Servings: 6 | Prep Time: 2 Hours 20 Minutes | Cook Time: 1 Hour

Ingredients

8 jumbo egg yolks

1/2 cup sugar plus more for topping

1 tsp. salt

1 tsp. culinary lavender

2 1/2 cups heavy whipping cream

Directions

1. Preheat your Anova Precision Cooker to 176F or 80C.

2. Combine the eggs, sugar, lavender, and salt, in a bowl and whisk them together.

3. Heat the cream on medium heat until simmering.

4. Carefully and slowly mix the cream into the lavender mixture using a whisk. Otherwise, the eggs will curdle.

5. Strain the ingredients and discard the lavender. Pour an equal amount of the mixture into 6 mason jars. Tighten the lids so they're finger tight.

6. Place the jars in your preheated container and set your Anova timer for 1 hour.

7. Once cooked, place the jars on a kitchen towel on the counter. Let the jars come down to room temperature.

8. Prepare an ice bath. Put the cooled jars in the ice bath until cold, top the crème brûlée with a layer of sugar and use a kitchen torch to caramelize it. Allow it harden for 5 minutes

9. Serve immediately.

Nutritional Info: Calories: 321, Sodium: 48 mg, Dietary Fiber: 0 g, Fat: 24.4 g, Carbs: 19 g, Protein 8.5 g

Classic Crème Brulee

This is your classic creamy crème brulee. You actually don't need to heat the cream in this thanks to the sous vide.

Servings: 6 | Prep Time: 2 Hours 20 Minutes | Cook Time: 1 Hour

Ingredients

11 egg yolks

granulated sugar, plus more for dusting

3 g salt

600 g heavy cream

6 (6-oz) mason jars

Directions

1. Preheat your Anova Precision Cooker to 176F or 80C.

2. Place the eggs, sugar, and salt, in a bowl and whisk them together.

3. Carefully and slowly mix the cream into the egg mixture using a whisk. Otherwise, the eggs will curdle.

4. Strain the new mixture and allow it to rest for 20-30 minutes. The goal is to get rid of all the bubbles. Take off any removing bubbles.

5. Slowly pour an equal amount of the mixture from a low height into the mason jars. You want to make sure you don't create more bubbles.

6. Tighten the lids so they're finger tight. You don't want to tighten the lids as tight as possible, because the trapped air may crack the jars.

7. Place the jars in your preheated container and set your Anova timer for 1 hour.

8. Once cooked, place the jars on a kitchen towel on the counter. Let the jars come down to room temperature.

9. Prepare an ice bath and place the cooled jars in the ice bath until cold.

10. Top the crème brulee with a layer of sugar using a sieve and use a kitchen torch to caramelize it. Allow it to harden for 5 minutes

11. Serve immediately.

Nutritional Info: Calories: 444, Sodium: 247 mg, Dietary Fiber: 0 g, Fat: 45.3 g, Carbs: 3.9 g, Protein 7 g

Leche Flan

This is a traditional Filipino Dessert that's incredibly rich with an amazing custard texture and caramel flavor.

Servings: 4 | Prep Time: 20 Minutes | Cook Time: 1 Hour

Ingredients

3/4 cups granulated sugar

12 egg yolks

1 (14-oz can) of condensed milk

1 (12-oz can) evaporated milk

1 tsp. vanilla extract

4 (1/2 pint) mason jars

Directions

1. Preheat your Anova Precision Cooker to 180F or 82C.

2. Heat the sugar in a saucepan on medium high heat. Stir constantly until the sugar melts and turns a caramel color. Pour equal portions of the caramel into the 4 mason jars and allow it cool

3. Lightly mix together the remaining ingredients and strain through cheesecloth. Pour an equal amount into the mason jars.

4. Place the jars in the preheated container and set your Anova timer for 2 hours.

5. When the flan is cooked, place the jars on a kitchen towel on the counter. Allow the jars to cool down to room temperature.

6. Place the jars in the refrigerator for at least 2 hours before serving.

7. Serve directly in the jar or remove and put the flan on a plate.

Nutritional Info: Calories: 665, Sodium: 212 mg, Dietary Fiber: 0 g, Fat: 26.6 g, Carbs: 89.6 g, Protein 19.9 g

Cinnamon Clove Banana Bowls

The bananas have a nice soft texture and brown sugar adds a rich sweetness. The cinnamon and cloves add spice and warmth.

Servings: 6 | Prep Time: 10 Minutes | Cook Time: 35 Minutes

Ingredients

7 ripe bananas

2 cinnamon sticks

1-1/4 cup brown sugar

6 cloves, whole

Directions

1. Preheat your Anova Precision Cooker to 176F or 80C. Peel the banana and slice it into chunks

2. Combine all the ingredients in a sous vide bag.

3. Place the bag in you preheated container and set your Anova timer for 35 minutes.

4. When the bananas are cooked, place them in 6 bowls and let them cool slightly.

5. Remove the cinnamon and cloves and serve alone or with ice cream.

Nutritional Info: Calories: 241, Sodium: 24 mg, Dietary Fiber: 7.1 g, Fat: 1.8 g, Carbs: 61 g, Protein 2 g

Sweet Corn Cheesecake

This cheesecake is easy to make and in perfect individual portions. It gets a nice sweetness from the corn.

Servings: 6 | Prep Time: 30 Minutes | Cook Time: 40 Minutes

Ingredients

1 cup frozen sweet corn

1/2 cup heavy cream

1/2 cup whole milk

4 eggs

1 cup sugar

1 tablespoon lemon juice

2 lemon peels

1/2 cup butter

3/4 cups cream cheese

3 ginger bread cookies

6 (6-oz) mason jars

Directions

1. Preheat your Anova Precision Cooker to 176F or 80C. Defrost the corn.

2. Place the first 6 ingredients in a blender and blend on high speed until smooth.

3. Add the mixture and the lemon peels to a sous vide bag.

4. Place the bag in your preheated container and set your Anova timer for 40 minutes.

5. When the mixture is cooked, discard the peels and place the mix back in the blender.

6. Add in the cream cheese and butter and blend on high until smooth. Allow the mixture to cool completely.

7. Pour an equal amount of the mixture in each mason jar. Crumble up the cookies and top each mason jar with the crumbs before serving.

Nutritional Info: Calories: 490, Sodium: 263 mg, Dietary Fiber: 1.2 g, Fat: 33.8 g, Carbs: 44.4 g, Protein 8 g

Classic Creamy Cheesecake

This is your classic cheesecake, but with the creamiest texture. You can serve as is or add your favorite toppings.

Servings: 5 | Prep Time: 15 Minutes | Cook Time: 90 Minutes

Ingredients

2 (8-oz) packages cream cheese

100 grams granulated sugar

2 grams Kosher salt

3 whole eggs

5 grams vanilla extract

130 grams buttermilk, or heavy whipping cream

5 (8-oz) mason jars

Directions

1. Preheat your Anova Precision Cooker to 176F or 80C. Allow the cream cheese to rise to room temperature.

2. Put the cream cheese, salt, and sugar in a food processor. Process until smooth, making sure you scrape the sides of the bowl throughout to ensure all ingredients are mixed.

3. Put in the eggs and vanilla and follow the same process as last time.

4. While the food processor is running, pour in the buttermilk. Continue to process until smooth. Strain the mixture through a fine mesh sieve for the smoothest texture. Pour an equal amount of mixture into each jar. Tighten the lids so they're finger tight.

5. Put the jars in your preheated container and set your Anova timer for 90 minutes.

6. When the cheesecake is cooked, place the jars on a kitchen towel on the counter. Let the jars come to room temperature. Refrigerate overnight.

7. Serve as is or with your favorite toppings.

Nutritional Info: Calories: 443, Sodium: 488 mg, Dietary Fiber: 0 g, Fat: 34.5 g, Carbs: 24 g, Protein 11 g

Bananas Foster

You'll never find an easier way to make bananas foster than this. The rum adds a delicious sweet and caramelized flavor to the bananas.

Servings: 2 | Prep Time: 15 Minutes | Cook Time: 25 Minutes

Ingredients

2 tbsp. dark rum

4 tbsp. butter

1 tsp. vanilla

1/2 cup brown sugar

2 bananas

1 tsp. cinnamon

1/2 cup pecans

2 scoops vanilla ice cream

Directions

1. Preheat your Anova Precision Cooker to 145F or 63C. Peel and cut the bananas into 1-inch pieces.

2. Place the vanilla, butter, brown sugar, and rum in a pan over high heat. Bring the mixture to a boil and remove from heat.

3. Season the bananas with cinnamon and put them in the bag of your choice with 3 tbsp. of the sauce.

4. Place the bag in your preheated container and set your Anova timer for 25 minutes.

5. When the bananas are cooked, plate them with a scoop of vanilla ice cream and top with the remaining sauce.

6. Serve immediately.

Nutritional Info: Calories: 722, Sodium: 228 mg, Dietary Fiber: 5.7 g, Fat: 40.4 g, Carbs: 81.7 g, Protein 5.4 g

Maple Raisin Rice Pudding with Ginger

Simply combine all the ingredients in a bag and let the sous vide do the work. The rice pudding is sweet thanks to the maple syrup and spicy thanks to the ginger.

Servings: 8 | Prep Time: 5 Minutes | Cook Time: 2 Hours

Ingredients

3 cups skim milk

2 tbsp. butter

2 cups Arborio rice

1/2 cup golden raisins

1/2 cup maple syrup

2 tsp. ground cinnamon

1/2 tsp. ground ginger

Directions

1. Preheat your Anova Precision Cooker to 180F or 82C.

2. Put all the ingredients in a sous vide bag and place the bag in your preheated container and set your Anova timer for 2 hours.

3. Once cooked, place equal portions in 8 bowls.

4. Top each bowl with a little extra cinnamon to serve.

Nutritional Info: Calories: 311, Sodium: 75 mg, Dietary Fiber: 2 g, Fat: 3.2 g, Carbs: 63.2 g, Protein 6.5 g

Caramelized Yogurt with Grilled Berries

This makes a healthy and delicious dessert. The yogurt has a nice caramelized flavor that goes well with the sweetness of the berries.

Servings: 8 | Prep Time: 1 Hour | Cook Time: 12 Hours

Ingredients

1 lb. natural yogurt plus 3.5 oz. natural yogurt

3.5 oz. blueberries

3.5 oz. raspberries

mint for garnish

Directions

1. Preheat your Anova Precision Cooker to 162F or 72C.

2. Place the yogurt in a sous vide bag and place the bag in the preheated container and set your timer for 12 hours.

3. When nearly finished cooking, prepare an ice bath.

4. Once cooked, place the bag in a bowl, and put the bowl in the ice bath. Allow the yogurt to cool.

5. Open the bag and pour the yogurt into a colander or sieve that's lined with muslin cloth. Position the sieve over a bowl and let strain for about an hour.

6. Slowly whisk in the 3.5 ounce of yogurt. Grill the berries on a very hot grill for a short time or heat with a kitchen torch. Garnish with mint to serve.

Nutritional Info: Calories: 101, Sodium: 48 mg, Dietary Fiber: 1.1 g, Fat: 3.5 g, Carbs: 10.8 g, Protein 5.4 g

Marsala Poached Pears with Cinnamon Mascarpone Whipped Cream

The Marsala adds a lovely chocolaty flavor, and the whipped cream balances out the rich flavors of the Marsala.

Servings: 4 | Prep Time: 25 Minutes | Cook Time: 1 Hours

Ingredients

4 Bartlett pears, peeled

1/2 cup Marsala wine

1 1/2 tsp. honey

2 tbsp. demerara sugar

1/3 cup mascarpone cheese

1/3 cup 35% whipping cream or coconut cream

1/4 tsp. ground cinnamon

1 tablespoon maple syrup or honey

Directions

1. Preheat your Anova Precision Cooker to 185F or 85C.

2. Place the first 4 ingredients in a sous vide bag. Then, place the bag in your preheated container and set your timer for 1 hour.

3. Towards the end of the cooking process, chill a bowl and place the cheese and cream in it. Whip the mixture until soft peaks appear. Whisk in the cinnamon and maple syrup until the peaks hold their shape.

4. When the pears are cooked, place them in a bowl and pour the juices into a pan. Heat on medium high heat until it reduces by half.

5. Pipe or place a dollop of whip cream on a plate with each pear. Top the pears with the warm sauce.

Nutritional Info: Calories: 259, Sodium: 26 mg, Dietary Fiber: 7 g, Fat: 7.7 g, Carbs: 42.5 g, Protein 3.6 g